AF522690

ENVIRONMENTAL AWARENESS ENVIRONMENTAL ATTITUDE AND ENVIRONMENTAL ETHICS OF TEACHER EDUCATION STUDENTS

ENVIRONMENTAL AWARENESS ENVIRONMENTAL ATTITUDE AND ENVIRONMENTAL ETHICS OF TEACHER EDUCATION STUDENTS

By

Dr. Shaik Fathima

M.Sc., M.A., M.Ed., M.Phil., Ph.D.

Teacher Educator

Bapuji College of Education

Tenali, Guntur Dist. (Andhra Pradesh)

(INDIA)

Editor

Prof. Digumarti Bhaskara Rao

M.Sc., M.A., M.A., M.Ed., Ph.D.

Dean, Faculty of Education

Former Chairman, Board of Studies in Education

Member, Standing Committee to Academic Senate

Member, Academic Senate

Acharya Nagarjuna University

D-43 (277) S.V.N. Colony

Guntur 522 006 (INDIA)

digumartibhaskararao@rediffmail.com

DISCOVERY PUBLISHING HOUSE PVT. LTD.

NEW DELHI-110 002

Published by:
Tilak Wasan
DISCOVERY PUBLISHING HOUSE PVT. LTD.
4383/4B, Ansari Road, Darya Ganj
New Delhi-110 002 (India)
Phone : +91-11-23279245, 43596064-65
Fax : +91-11-23253475
E-mail : discoverypublishinghouse@gmail.com
sales@discoverypublishinggroup.com
parul.wasan@gmail.com
web : www.discoverypublishinggroup.com

***First Edition:* 2014**

ISBN: 978-93-5056-442-4

Environmental Awareness, Environmental Attitude and Environmental Ethics of Teacher Education Students

Printed at:
Dynamic Printers
Delhi

FOREWORD

Environmental education serves as a common thread uniting long standing interests and emphasizing nature study, conservation education and outdoor education. It is characterized by the development of explicit and implicit interconnection with human health, science and technology, and also the environmental, economic, and social issues and problems of the society.

Environmental awareness is the sensitivity to the total environment and its allied problems. The development of environmental awareness means to understand the environmental problems and to develop critical thinking and problem solving skill in the people. Teachers can play a pivotal role in transmitting knowledge and creating awareness about the environment and help to tackle the local and global environmental issues. The teacher's community should be motivated and committed to the cause of realising the goals of environmental education and should take initiatives in designing the programme of environmental education.

Environmental attitude means to acquire a set of values and feelings of concern for the environment and the motivation of active participation in environmental improvement and protection. Environmental knowledge and awareness would be of no meaning without cultivation of right attitude towards environment. So, attitude is a pre-requisite for fostering valuing approach and responsible action which is ultimate goal of environmental education.

Environmental ethics is the scientific study of various issues related to the rights of the individual with regard to the environment. It is the moral relationship of human beings with the environment and the responsibility to understand the environmental consequence of our consumption and need to recognise our individual and social responsibility to conserve natural resources and protect the earth for future generation.

Environmental awareness, environmental attitude and environmental ethics of teacher education students make them to introduce innovative methods, strategies and techniques of teaching environmental education. Hence, it is intended to measure the environmental awareness, environmental attitude and environmental ethics of teacher education students and the association among environmental awareness, environmental attitude and environmental ethics. The teacher education students had average environmental awareness and environmental ethics and high environmental attitude.

Digumarti Bhaskara Rao
digumartibhaskararao@rediffmail.com
Tele-mobile: +91 949 3333 555 & 8500114411

CONTENTS

1

INTRODUCTION

Science is one of those human activities that can be created to gratify certain human needs and desires. In our modern world, science should be regarded as a 'way of life' or 'philosophy of living' because the whole of the universe is being dominated by the application of science. Science is progressing at an unimaginary speed and has surpassed all the miracles of mythology. There is not even a single area which is left out by the magic touch of science. By exploiting the inquisitive nature of man, science goes on changing minute by minute and constructing new knowledge day-by-day.

Since science is an advancing subject, students are finding it hard to cope with the immense amount of data that is being generated. The teachers too must devise new strategies and methods to assimilate the scientific knowledge and disseminate it among his students. The known knowledge of the teacher about the concerned subject must be presented as a problem before the students from which they must be able to derive solutions and such an experience will lead the students to know about the unknown.

While learning science, the students should be able to solve problems independently and to apply the theories learnt in practical situations. He should develop a scientific attitude, interest and curiosity. We cannot develop these qualities only by giving factual information. Science students should be considered as little scientists working in laboratories. The teacher should guide and lead students to discoveries and to solve problems. This is the first step to scientific literacy. Students gain a lot by doing experiments individually and also in groups. The task of science teachers is to develop and experiment new strategies which will help the students to acquire the ever increasing knowledge of science.

Environmental Science

Environmental Science can be defined as the science that deals with the inter-relationship between organisms and their environment. A close interaction occurs between life and the environment in which it exists. For example, the environment of a plant includes the soil, water, minerals, nutrients and the air in the immediate vicinity. Rainfall and temperature affect the life of the plant and so do the plants, which are present around it and compete for water, food and other resources. All these constitute the plant's environment. The exchange of gases and nutrients affect and modify the environment. There are animals which eat the plant and others which help it to reproduce. The science which deals with the ways in which plants and animals (biota) affect their environment and are affected by it, is called environmental science. (Mukherjee, 1997).

Environmental Education

Good environmental education like any good education, must lead students out and from their immediate perceptions and experiences to a wider understanding, which must develop their capacity and this cannot happen by chance. A number of subjects and aspects of the school curriculum deal with matters to do with the interplay between man and his environment. Pupil must first learn about natural phenomena in order to understand complex environmental matters. The environmental education sensitizes us to the causes and effects of problems of which for long, we have been only dimly aware. The environment involves our children's future and many already know that they must encourage them to think positively about it. (Ghante, 1998).

Environmental education, today, serves as a common thread uniting long standing interests and emphasizing nature study, conservation education and outdoor education. Environmental education has also been characterized by the development of explicit and implicit interconnection with human health, science and technology, and the environmental, economic, and social issues and problems of the society. It is generally accepted that increased concern for environmental quality and fear of severe deterioration of human health and quality of human life caused by dramatic decline in environmental quality, gave impetus for synthesis leading to environmental education. Every individual has the right to seek a healthy environment to live in. It makes the environmental awareness and environmental education internationally imperative. (Chanda, 2000).

The most hazardous event of the 21st century is the rapid degradation of environmental quality. The population explosion creates situations like more people needs more food, more energy, and more things of daily use, such as housing, clothing and automobiles. As a result, we use more water resources, fertilizers and pesticides for more production and in turn, increase the level of air pollution, water pollution besides disturbing the ecological balance. All these conditions cause diseases and deaths in many species of animals, birds and human beings. Similarly, the indiscriminate use of renewable and non-renewable physical resources leads to severe difficulties.

Lack of environmental awareness about preservation and conservation of environment effectively add fuel to fire. All these are greatly responsible for rapid degradation of the environmental quality at grass root level and similar situations in various spheres. At this juncture, the only alternative is to create environmental awareness among the people in respect of protection, preservation, conservation of environment and also for the mitigation of environmental degradation. All these are possible only through envirsonmental education.

Environmental education should result in the development of an ecological ethic and enable the individual and the society to perceive environment in its totality and integrate physical, biological, technological, socio-cultural, moral, economic, historical and aesthetic components. In a country like India where 76 per cent of its population lives in rural areas, environmental education is very much necessary to protect our environment and to attain sustainable development.

The crucial aim of environmental education is the development of behaviour which is in accordance with environmental needs. This means to transfer our knowledge and experience into everyone's life. Therefore, environmental education should be related to the problems as they exist in the pupil. (Vashist, 2003).

An environmental education programme based on a sound pedagogical basis should be directed towards achieving the following objectives formulated in Tibilsi Conference, 1975. (UNESCO/UNEP, Intergovernmental Conference).

1. *Awareness:* To develop individuals and social groups, acquire an awareness and sensitivity to the total environment and its associated problems.
2. *Knowledge:* To help individuals and social groups, acquire basic understanding of the total environment, its associated problems and humanity's critically responsible presence and role in it.
3. *Attitude:* To help individuals and social groups, acquire social values, strong feelings of concern for the environment and motivation to actively participate in its protection and improvement.
4. *Skills:* To help individuals and social groups, acquire the knowledge and skills of solving environmental problems.
5. *Evaluation Ability:* To help individuals and social groups, evaluate environmental measures and educational programmes in terms of ecological, political, economical, social, aesthetic and educational factors.
6. *Participation:* To help individuals and social groups, develop a sense of responsibility and urgency regarding environmental problems to ensure appropriate action for solving the problems.

The spectrum of environmental education falls in four major but integrating components: *(i)* awareness, *(ii)* real life situations, *(iii)* conservation and *(v)* sustainable development. This has to be watched with the needs of primary, lower secondary, higher secondary and tertiary or the adult education. (Khoshoo, 1991).

The goal of environmental education is to develop world population that is aware of and concerned about the environment and its associated problems which has the knowledge, skills, attitudes, motivation and commitment to work individually and collectively towards solution of current problems and prevention of new ones (Saxena, 1996). Environmental education is indeed very important to child and adult for self-fulfilment and social development. It helps in the maintenance of life and health, in self-preservation and in the preservation of human race (Rao and Reddy, 1997).

Environmental education is a pragmatic response to the havoc wrecked on the environment. It makes pupil fully aware of the problems connected with their environment and motivates them to tackle these problems with a sense of responsibility and with the technical skills, which enable them to contribute to their solutions along with other members of their community.

The environmental education movement in India has started only in the later phase of the 20th century. NCERT did pioneering work in environmental education by not only developing a modern curriculum for formal school system that incorporates environmental education concept, but also prepared text books and other instructional material, teaching aids and audiovisual materials. The centre for Environmental Education (CEE), Ahmedabad is involved in increasing the consciousness about the environment among children and the general community.

It is our foremost duty to conserve our environmental resources. The ultimate goal of environmental education, whether it is formal or non-formal, is to create awareness among the citizens of a country. The basic aim of environmental education is, "To develop a world population that is aware of and concerned about the environment, its associated problems, so that the population will have the knowledge, skill, attitude, motivation and commitment to work individually and collectively towards the solutions of current problems and prevention of new ones". (UNESCO-UNEP IEEP Environmental Education, Series 6, 1985).

Global concern regarding the steadily deteriorating state of environment has emphasized the need for environmental education obviously a powerful vehicle bringing about change, a panacea of all evils and a potent weapon for prevention that plays a central role in the society. The need of the hour is to make people sensitive towards nature through a strong programme of environmental education (Nachimuthu and Kumari, 1993). Environmental education is a way of creating knowledge, understanding, values, attitudes, skills, abilities and awareness among individual and social groups towards the environmental protection.

Environmental education is an attempt to reorient education so that environmental competence is restored as one of its basic aim along with personal and social competence. It is not just a subject of education but an expansion of its whole philosophy recognising our environment as continuous with ourselves and in need of the same care and understanding we give to our personal and social well-being (Smyth, 1995). World educators and environmental specialists have repeatedly pointed out that a solution to environmental awareness and its proper understanding should deeply root in the education system at all levels of school education (Shukla, 2001). The existing curricula at primary, secondary and college level provide a lot of opportunities to make the students aware of environment. The integration of environmental education is possible if the teacher has a will to introduce it in a quiet natural way while teaching different curricular areas at primary, secondary and higher education levels.

Teachers and students jointly explore the aspects of problem rather than teacher telling the students about the solution of the problem. The need for radical changes in educational technology for keeping up with the increasing volume and variety of knowledge, is being recognised as an inevitable phenomenon in the changing process of secondary education in India. Several instructional procedures and self-learning materials are being used today for imparting instructions at the individual level.

Education and Environment

People while dealing with nature and natural resources have accumulated a lot of empirical knowledge on the basis of their experiences. This is based on the intrinsic relation that man and nature form part of an indivisible whole, therefore people in traditional societies developed an eco-centric view, which is widely reflected in their attitudes towards plants, animals, rivers and the earth. All this knowledge of man is communicated in different ways to the next generation. This knowledge has been termed as "Traditional Ecological Knowledge" (TEK). According to Ramakrishnan (2001), benefits of TEK are of three kinds:

1. *Economic* – plants and animals of food value, medicinal plants, etc.
2. *Ecological/Social* – manipulation of bio-diversity for controlling soil, water and hydrology for efficient organic residue management, soil fertility management, through modified soil/biological process, etc., and
3. *Ethical* – cultural, spiritual and religious belief system centered around concept of sacred species, severed groves and sacred landscapes.

Since ancient times, this knowledge has been communicated through three types of education, *i.e.*

(i) *Formal* – well designed and planned education given through schools, colleges, universities, etc.

(ii) *Non-formal* – any organized, systematic educational activity outside the framework of formal system, for example - through mass-media, open education system, etc. and

(iii) *Informal* – any incidental learning in family, at workplace, during travel, etc.

Therefore, education, in its various forms, has been used to create, conserve and transfer knowledge from time to time. At the same time, education has been used to develop human potential for his/her 'self-development' and also for making him useful for the society. It has been rightly said in National Policy on education (1986) that "Education is an investment in present and future". So, for betterment of present environment and to hand over that better environment to future generations, environmental concerns must be incorporated at all levels of education, *i.e.*

(i) Pre-primary,
(ii) Primary,
(iii) Secondary and
(iv) Tertiary level of education.

Steps in this direction have been initiated in the form of environmental education worldwide since 1970s.

Goals of Environmental Education in Teacher Education

- To provide every teacher educator with opportunities to acquire knowledge, values, attitudes, commitment and skills needed to protect and improve the environment.
- To foster clear awareness of and concern about economic, social, political and ecological interdependence in urban and rural teacher training institutions.
- To create new patterns of behaviour of individual groups and society as a whole towards the environment.

Objectives of Environmental Education in Teacher Education

- *Awareness:* To help teacher educators and teacher trainees gain a variety of experience with the total environment to acquire a basic understanding of the total environment, its associated problems and humanity's critical responsible presence and role in it.
- *Attitude:* To help teacher educators and teacher trainees acquire social values for working towards the solution of environmental problems and to foster a dialogue between these groups.

- *Skills*: To help teacher educators and teacher trainees for working towards the solution of environmental problems and to foster a dialogue between these groups.
- *Participation;* To help teacher educators and teacher trainees develop a sense of responsibility and urgency regarding environmental problems to ensure appropriate action to help solve these problems.

Guiding Principles of Environmental Education in Teacher Education

- Environmental education should consider environment in its totality.
- Environmental education should be a life-long process.
- Environmental education should be inter-disciplinary in its approach. It should be considered a new approach to education. It should examine major environmental issues from local, national, regional and international points of view.
- Environmental education should focus on current and potential environmental situation which takes into account the historical perspective. It should also be considered that responses to situational needs vary between and within countries.
- Environmental education should focus on complexity of environmental problems and develop critical thinking and problem solving skills.
- Environmental education should utilise variety of learning environments and educational approaches to teaching/learning with lots of practical activities.

Teaching Methodology for Environmental Education in Teacher Education

Before adopting any methodology of teaching any lesson/ unit related to 'Environmental Education', it is most important to decide the 'Instructional Objectives' or 'Intended Learning Outcomes' or 'Performance Objectives'.

It is also important to note that student teachers should be taught about the 'environment, from the environment and for the environment'. Some of the methods of teaching Environmental Education can be as follows:

- Use of traditional modes of interaction such as folklore, folk art, puppetry, etc.
- Use of traditional media should be supplemented by Textbooks, Reference books, Pamphlets, etc.
- Use of only print materials.
- Use of modern media like TV, VCR, different types of projectors, etc., here, multimedia approach is followed.
- Learner-centered and activity-oriented approaches involve individual and group-centered activities, where activity is assigned by the teacher. Later on, group leaders/ group members share their experiences through discussions.
- Organization of group discussions, workshops, seminars, etc.
- Out-of-classroom experiences like visits to school/college campus, the neighbourhood post office, bank, grocery store, zoo, museum, park, near by ponds, fields and other such public places, variety of places of human activity, variety of human habitations and variety of natural habitats.
- Innovative teaching-learning strategies like role-playing, simulation exercise, case studies and other new teaching strategies can be taught and implemented by teacher.

Evaluation Procedures in Environmental Education

Evaluation is done on the basis of instructional objectives which were operationally defined in behaviour terms in the beginning itself. Clearly and specifically stated objectives make the evaluation procedure quite easy. However, in case of Environmental Education, development of cognitive, affective as well as psychomotor domain is required. Development of last two domains is more important; but, at the same time, its evaluation is a difficult work. Therefore, evaluation in Environmental Education is complex as compared to other subjects. Some evaluation procedures are as follows:

- *Teacher's Observation:* For assessing skills, attitudes and values, observation records should be maintained.
- *Teacher-made Tests*: These may be oral or written (objective type, short answer type or essay type). These tests may also be in the form of situation-reaction tests.
- *Pupils Records*: In the form of their observation and writings. Besides this, a record of assessment of pupils by teacher should also be maintained.
- *Questionnaires and Interview Schedules*: To obtain results from students, peers, parents and other community members.
- *Rating Scales, Check Lists*: Analysis of student's product, sociometry can be used for measuring students attitude towards environmental issues and actions.
- Other innovative procedures can also be used by teacher.

Environmental crisis is the greatest crisis of the day. Educational intervention through informal, non-formal and informal settings can be one important remedy. But, the initiative regarding implementation of Environmental Education programme has to be taken by educational institutions. Universities must take a lead in this area by framing suitable programmes for Environmental Education, personal training, material preparation for Environmental Education and execution of the whole programme in a proper way. The whole question is of 'values'. How it should be done? It is your turn to 'think and act'.

Environmental Education at School Level

At the formative stage of education (6-11 years), the approach to environmental education can be very varied. The approach should be to integrate the learning of the various subjects of the primary curriculum so that concern for the actual environment gives realism to the subject concerned. Environmental education should appeal to the children's sensory facilities. Training of primary school teachers and giving them opportunity to study their environment under guidance.

Environmental Education at secondary school level will have to emphasize the local environment. In should be interdisciplinary. Emphasis should be given to the problem of solving and responsiveness to the community. Necessary training and information should be provided to the students for the protection of natural environment. Out-of-school activities through eco-development camps have to be encouraged for imparting the integrated knowledge of environment.

The environment education at tertiary level should be provided by colleges, universities, research institutions, institutes of planning and management, agricultural, medical and engineering universities, etc. The major aim of university environmental education at the professional level is to help the students in developing a broad conceptual framework. It is to develop specialized knowledge which can be achieved through the introduction of courses and research programme in environmental studies.

Outline of Environmental Education

To spread the knowledge of environmental education, planned environmental education will have to be introduced from primary level. The outline of environmental education could be as follows:

1. Childhood is the time when the child's basic outlooks, values and habits are shaped to a great extent. The experiences which the child has at school and at home, in these formative years, determine the behaviour of the child. The young children have great curiosity about their surroundings. They possess great love for nature and want to understand myths and mysteries of nature. Therefore, at this stage, stress should lay on developing an emotional tie with nature. Method of teaching should be used as to cultivate love for nature. As children mature, they become more conscious of social relationships, of civic responsibility, of moral values and they like to participate in community programmes.
2. These children have a broader experience and logical thinking. A few lessons on concept of environment and environmental balance with its need and importance, and

effects of environmental misbalance should be included in the syllabus. These concepts can be explained and be given a practical touch involving the children in civic programmes, such as plantation of trees, maintenance of garden, meeting with the people of slums and near by areas to promote civic awareness. 'Environmental Science' should be introduced at undergraduate and postgraduate levels. Several new courses at both levels should be introduced in science, engineering, commerce and arts such as, environment and development, agriculture and environment, chemical implications of air pollution, waste water treatment, industry and environment, production through waste material, etc., production of electricity from the waste is now becoming popular. This solves the problem of disposal of waste as well as providing fuel for electricity generation. Project work, at post-graduate level that usually forms part of these courses, can provide good opportunities for useful investigations related to environment. Projects as a survey of environmental awareness among teachers, effects of pollution on health, etc., can be undertaken. Moreover, researches exploring the condition of environment, factors polluting environment, effectiveness of various measures used in different industries for controlling pollution and their after – effects should get full attention.

3. Co-curricular activities like scouting, NCC, NSS should become part of school curriculum. Volunteers can make attempts to promote environmental awareness through several activities like plays, songs, talking with people, tree plantation, maintenance of healthy environment, etc.
4. The teacher plays an important role in shaping and impounding the habits, tastes, manners and good character of the children. Therefore, to gear up environmental awareness programme, it is essential that teachers should have sufficient knowledge of environmental education. It is the responsibility of teacher education colleges and universities to groom

teachers for this task too. The existing teacher education courses (Nursery or pre-school, B.Ed., M.Ed., in-service teachers training) should be suitably amended to incorporate environmental education content emphasizing methods to deal with environmental education content at school and college and to develop skills in organizing environmental education programmes with curricular activities.

5. There is a need of mass awareness about environment. Millions of people are unaware of the beauty and wealth of nature. They just enjoy the comfort gifted by nature to them. Everyone can do something for saving and enriching the environment. In fact, we do not know how grave the problems are and how we are sharing in polluting the integration of three approaches to environmental education which have commonly become known as 'education in the environment, education about the environment, and education for the environment'.

Education in the Environment

Experience in the environment – it may be a city street or a farm, a rural village or an island beach, a park or a forest – can be used to give reality, relevance and practical experience to learning. Increased awareness of aspects of the environment can be expected from any opportunities for direct contact with the environment. Opportunities to learn out-of-doors can also be used to develop important skills for data gathering, such as observation, sketching, photography, interviewing, and using scientific instruments, and social skills such as group work, co-operation and aesthetic appreciation. Environmental awareness and concern can also be fostered by linking learning to direct experiences in the environment and allowing learners to become captivated by the complexity and wonder of natural systems or immersed in the values conflict over particular environmental issues. One commentator has summarized the central thrust of education in the environment as 'education for environmental awareness and interpretation' as a result of these benefits (Huckle 1993).

Education about the Environment

Awareness and feelings of concern for the environment are not enough, however, if living responsibly and sustainably in the environment is one of the educational goals. Concerned needs to be translated into appropriate behaviour patterns and actions but, for this to happen in an informed and responsible way. It is necessary for learners to have a basic understanding of how natural systems work and the impact of human activities upon them. This will include learning about political, economic and socio-cultural factors, as well as about the ecological ones that influence decisions about how to responsibly use the environment. Attitude about the environment is essential if all citizens are to participate in any informed debate aimed at resolving local, national and global environmental issues. As a result of these objectives, Huckle (1993) has described the central thrust of education about the environment as "education for environmental management".

Education for the Environment

Education for the environment aims to promote a willingness and ability to adopt lifestyles that are compatible with the wise use of environmental resources. In doing so, it builds on education in and about the environment to help and develop an informed concern and sense of responsibility for the environment through the development of an environmental ethic and the motivation and skills necessary to participate in environmental improvement. The UNESCO-UNEP International Environmental Education Programme has stressed that environmental education needs to be based upon a search for answers to a number of critical questions.

International Recognition for Teacher Education in Environmental Education

Since 1970, a great number of both international and intergovernmental organizations and agencies have recognised the urgent need to develop environmental education in teacher education programmes. This has been documented in many conferences, such as the International Union for the Conservation of Nature and Natural Resources (IUCN) 'Environmental Education' Conference (1971), the

International Belgrade Workshop (1975), the Tbilisi Conference (1977) and the most recent United Nations Conference on Environment and Development, the Earth Summit (1992).

At an IUCN conference held in Switzerland in 1971, the representatives of over a hundred countries highlighted the importance of teacher education:

Teacher training forms one of the most important and significant aspects in the development of environmental education programmes and recommend that:

(a) The training of teachers provides them with essential basic knowledge of ecological facts and an adequate background of sociology and its relationship to human ecology.

(b) Efforts should be made to develop in teachers a critical awareness of environmental problems to enable them to provoke responsible attitudes concerning environmental matters in their pupils.

(c) Environmental conservation is recognised as an essential part of the teacher training and that developments started in pre-service training should be continued by in-service training.

(d) As teacher training in environmental education involves the use of many techniques and methods, all prospective teachers should be given training in the use and evaluation of pedagogic methods, including those relating to inter-disciplinary approaches and team teaching.

The National Policy on Education – 1986, revised in 1992, states that "There is a paramount need to create a consciousness of the environment and it must permeate all ages and all sections of society, beginning with the child." It has also been highlighted in the National Curriculum Framework for School Education – 2000 that the Environmental Education be included at all levels of schooling.

1. Environmental Awareness

Environment has been defined as "the sum total of all conditions and influences that affect the development and life of an organism". Ecologists divide the environment into three parts:

1. Physical surroundings/Abiotic environment.
2. Living organisms/Biotic environment.
3. Meteorological factors/Climatic factors.

The uncontrolled activities of human beings are damaging the healthy environment more and more. There are some environmental problems where priority action is needed. They are:

1. Population stabilization,
2. Integrated land use planning,
3. Healthy crop land and grass land,
5. Conservation of biological diversity,
6. Control of water and air pollution,
7. Development of non-polluting renewable energy systems,
8. Recycling of wastes and residues,
9. Human settlement,
10. Environmental education and awareness; updating environmental laws, and
11. New dimensions of natural security.

These are the important issues that are posing threat to our environment as a whole and to sustainability in particular. Now, the understanding of the ecology and environmental awareness is essential for the wise management of the planets.

Environmental awareness is a dynamic process that can help to reduce and solve some of the problems of environmental degradation faced by the countries of the region. Rather than establishing a new subject called environmental studies, most countries are presently infusing environmental education objectives and strategies into existing curricula. This is viewed as strength because the content of environmental education is relevant to the themes in many learning areas such as social studies and science, and duplication can be prevented. In addition, the focus on practical learning in the real world in environmental education help schools address important general education objectives related to values and to skill development.

The environment for man is earth. It alone contains man, animals and plants. Now, the earth has become sick by the activities of man. The united nations conference on environment and development held in Rio De Janerio on 1992, known as 'Earth Summit' followed by the world summit on sustainable development at Johannesburg in 2002 and in December 2009, in Danish Capital 'The Copenhagen summit' has brought the issue of rapid environmental degradation and climate change on to the centre stage and have highlighted the key issue of global environment concern and have attracted the attention of general public towards the deteriorating environment. Any government as its own level can not achieve the goal of sustainable development until the public has a participatory role in it. Public participation should be made aware about the environmental issues.

Environmental management has become a part of the health care sector and managing environmental hazards and preventing possible disasters has become an urgent need. An intellectual property right has become important in a bio-diversity-rich country like India to protect microbes, plants and animals that have useful genetic properties. No other country in earth has created environmental awareness by infusing newer pro-environmental concepts into formal curricular processes. Remember, environment protection begins with 'I and You'.

An emerging trend in the integration of environment, population and development education in several countries is a reflection of national policies in these fields and to see education contributing to the integration of national, social, cultural and economic goals. Thus, nature study and the management of natural resources such as forests, water, sea, etc., are no longer the only aspect of environmental studies. Besides these concerns, environmental education, now, can focus on ways of improving the quality of life of all people, rich and poor. These issues often relate to housing, sanitation, hygiene, health, waste management, energy, population and security of access to life essentials such as water, food, shelter, work, transport, drugs, health and recreation.

In some countries, nationally determined syllabi provide for a coordinated programme of environmental topics in both primary and secondary schools. Some other countries have developed environmental education guidelines which support schools and teachers. However, there is, unfortunately, often a lack of co-ordination in several countries in the national environmental education framework which prevents the development of a comprehensive environmental education programme for all students. This means that all countries in the region suffer from some of the following barriers to environmental education at some levels of education at various times.

- Some rigidity of syllabus and examination process.
- A strong disciplinary orientation and inflexible time tables, especially in secondary schools.
- A lack of up-to-date topical local materials, especially of a visual type.
- Little co-ordination between government departments and between government departments and NGOs.
- Little co-ordination between schools and their local communities.
- A lack of pre-service and in-service teacher education in environmental education.

Environmental Awareness issues in teacher education could include:

1. An increasing and widening of interest in environmental education across the range of disciplines in teacher education.
2. A sharing of expertise, debate and research in environmental education across teacher education institutions.
3. An identification of the competencies required of the environmentally educated teacher.
4. A review of existing provission for environmental education in teacher education programmes.
5. Comprehensive approach to preparing teachers for the challenges and responsibilities they face in environmental education in schools and colleges.

Much of the focus, however, is on pre-service teacher education because of the need to address the importance of environmental education in teachers' work right from the beginning of their professional socialization and training. However, relevant to the in-service professional associations, education systems and schools are invited to consider these implications for their initiatives in the fields of curriculum preparation, staff development, short courses, higher degree studies, and research in environmental education.

The Environment Education and Training Scheme, developed by Government of India, is precisely meant for environmental awareness. Under this scheme, various programmes are conducted every year for creating environmental awareness both through non-formal activities as well as through formal education system. While the programmes like National Environmental Awareness Campaign (NEAC) and National Green Corps (NGC), which use of Electronic Media, etc., fall in the non-formal sector; the project for strengthening environmental concept in the school curriculum and the Global Learning and Observations to Benefit the Environment (GLOBE) programme use the formal education system for conveying the message.

Central and State Government Policies

The National Council of Educational Research and Training outlined the concept of environment education in different publications in 1975, for example, "Curriculum for the Ten-Year School: A Framework". These documents emphasized that the child's learning experiences should be derived from the disciplines of sciences in general and biology in particular. As a result of these recommendations, Environmental studies (EVS) was introduced, by integrating the science and social science curricula. Environmental studies is used as an interdisciplinary subject in the initial years of schooling. Hence, NCERT, as per directions of Hon'ble Supreme Court of India, designed the syllabi of environmental education for different classes, which emphasize the emotional and attitudinal aspects of learners' personality along with the requisite cognitive component. It is a value based and action oriented syllabus that would lead from knowledge to feeling and finally to appropriate action. The syllabus of environmental education at this level aims at generating among learners an awareness and sensitivity to the total environment in a holistic manner and the problems associated with it.

University Grants Commission, India organized a National Seminar on 'Environmental Education through Universities' in 1984. The outcome of the seminar was that in spite of all members recognising the importance of environment education, only few were clear on measures to be adopted for the same. Few have any idea or experience as how environment education can be successfully taught. UGC has developed a six months compulsory core module course in Environmental Studies, which is integrated into the teaching programmes of all undergraduate courses. The course comprises 50 lectures, of which 45 lectures are done in the class room and 5 lectures are covered through field activities. The course material is provided by UGC for both classroom and field activities. Evaluation is through examinations conducted at the end of the semester and is worth 100 marks, of which 25 marks are for field work. The Indira Gandhi National Open University has also launched awareness level courses of study in environment and also a Post Graduate Diploma in Environment and Sustainable Development.

Green Teacher, a distance education course in environment education, for practicing teachers is a one year diploma programme for teachers and educators. Initially the course was offered through the print medium compiled in four modules, supported by field assignments and contact classes, now the programme is also being offered both online and off-line with a suitable Learning Management System.

The Green Teacher programme was an outcome of India's National Policy of Education (1986) and the Supreme Court ruling of 2003 that environment education should be a compulsory curricular component at all levels of education, starting 2004-05. The Green teacher programme develops the necessary knowledge, skills and ideas pertaining to environment in the practicing teachers, which is a novel initiative taking into consideration their constraints at the workplace. The Centre for Science and Environment, New Delhi, India has launched a Green Schools Programme in which 'survey' of the school done by a school on its environmental practices called environmental auditing. The students form teams and explore the status of water, energy, land, air and waste in the school. The teacher is a facilitator and organizes activities on the basis of a handbook called the Green Schools Programme Manual. The Environment Education Unit (EEU) of the centre conducts a two-day training programme for teachers, educators, development workers and people interested in environment education. The training includes interactive sessions, film presentations and several modules on how they can implement the environment programmes in their schools.

A Green Educators Network has been launched which has the vision of bringing together the environment educators across the world to create a forum to share and discuss various aspects of environmental education. It had also released 'Down to Earth', a weekly dispatch of feature articles in English and Hindi language.

Formal Environment Education

The Government of India, Ministry of Education has taken various initiatives for strengthening Environment Education (EE) in the formal curriculum. For this purpose, the government had been closely interacting with the University Grants Commission (UGC), the National Council of Education Research and Training (NCERT), the Ministry of Human Resources Development (MHRD), the All India Council for Technical Education (AICTE) and the State Education Departments to ensure integration of environmental concept into the curriculum.

Some of the initiatives undertaken in environmental education are explained here under.

Pilot Project on Environment Education in School System (EESS)

This project was earlier launched with the basic objective of strengthening Environmental Education in the formal school system. During Phase I, a nation wide survey to assess the extent of its delivery in the classroom was conducted by Bharatiya Vidyapeeth Institute for Environmental Education and Research (BVIEER). As a part of this study, a national consultation on EE was organized that was of the view that instead of teaching environment as a separate subject, separate space/forum should be created within the school system for integrating various environmental concepts infused/ introduced in other subjects. Based on these recommendations and the outcomes of the EE study carried out by the BVIEER, the EESS project was implemented in eight States, namely: *(i)* Andhra Pradesh, *(ii)* Assam, *(iii)* Goa, *(iv)* Jammu and Kashmir, *(v)* Maharashtra, *(vi)* Orissa, *(vii)* Punjab and *(viii)* Uttaranchal on a pilot basis under Phase II of the project. One hundred schools in each of these states were selected for pilot implementation. During the pilot implementation, the textbooks of Science, Social Studies and language of standards VI to VIII in the selected schools of the project States were modified to strengthen infusion of environmental education on the basis of findings of Phase I study. This exercise was also accompanied by development of other education material like teachers' handbooks/guides/manuals, classroom materials, etc. Subsequently, the concerned teachers (about five in number) from each project school were also trained for effectively teaching environmental concept infused in the modified/greened textbooks. The modified textbooks were introduced in the project schools.

In view of the success of this initiative, the project was extended until 30th June, 2004 and seven additional States, *viz.*, Chhattisgarh, Himachal Pradesh, Karnataka, Kerala, Sikkim, Tamil Nadu, and Tripura were covered. Hundred schools from each of these States implemented the project on pilot basis as done previously for the eight States. Activities like development and printing of educational materials including textbooks, training of master trainers, training of teachers, introduction of green textbooks in the project schools, etc., were completed in the seven States.

Global Learning and Observation to Benefit Environment (GLOBE)

GLOBE is an international science and education programme, which provides 'Hand-on Environmental learning' of environmental concepts to the students to carry out various measurements so that they can learn about scientific protocol and perform environmental learning activities, which have already been introduced as theory in the greened textbooks developed for EESS project. These experiments and measurement were included as a part of new curriculum so that the students can gain a better understanding of the infused environmental contents by taking measurement and doing practicals. The Hands-on Environmental Learning programme, being an integral component of EESS project, has been implemented in all the EESS project schools.

About 1800 teachers from about 1700 schools have been trained in various protocols for conducting the experiments in respect of four broad environmental parameters, namely: *(i)* hydrology, *(ii)* soil, *(iii)* land cover and *(vi)* atmospheric temperature/rainfall. Instruments/kits for carrying out various experiments have been provided to about 800 schools. While more than 400 schools have already started taking the measurement, more than 200 schools are regularly reporting the data collected by them.

Strengthening Environment Education in Indian Management Schools

This initiative, which was launched by the Ministry of Environment, integrates environmental concepts in the management education, made a good progress. An inventory of the courses offered in India and abroad has been prepared along with the inventory of resource material.

Environment Appreciation Courses

In order to provide interested persons an opportunity to learn in detail about specific environmental issues, the Ministry of Environment and Forests, Government of India has already got a course module developed from Indira Gandhi National Open University (IGNOU) for Environmental Appreciation courses. It proposed to start delivery of these courses through distance education mode by IGNOU. IGNOU has started introducing these courses at the under graduate level on compulsory basis.

Non-formal Environment Education and Awareness

Environmental education, awareness and training play a significant role in encouraging and enhancing people's participation in activities aimed at conservation, protection and management of the environment, essential for achieving sustainable development. Accordingly, the Ministry of Environment and Forests accords priority to the promotion of non-formal environmental education and creation of awareness among all sections of the society through diverse activities using traditional and modern media of communication.

National Environment Awareness Campaign (NEAC)

The NEAC programme was started in 1986 for creating environmental awareness at national level. An action component was introduced in the awareness campaign. This programme was continued during the year 1986 with the main theme as 'Solid Waste Management'. The following sub themes for action components were considered for financial assistance:

- Household waste and composting/vermi-composting.
- Municipal waste.
- Bio-medical waste.
- Plastic waste.
- Waste management at higher altitude.
- Electronic waste (e-waste).
- Industrial waste including fly ash.

Twenty nine organizations located in different parts of the country, designated as Regional Resource Agencies (RRAs) by the Ministry of Environment and Forests, implemented NEAC programme for 2004-05 and physically monitored the activities in the areas of their jurisdiction.

Seven thousand five hundred and eighty eight participating organizations were provided financial assistance for organizing awareness creating activities such as padayatras, rallies, public meetings, exhibitions, folk dances, street theaters, essay/debate, painting/poster, competitions for school children, seminars, workshops, training courses, etc., for preparation and distribution of environmental education resource material and for following these with action oriented activities. Diverse target groups ranging from students/youth/teachers to tribal, rural population, professionals, etc., were covered under the campaign.

National Green Corps (Eco-clubs)

To impart environmental education and to encourage and mobilize participation of school children in various environmental conservation activities in the localities, the Ministry of Environment and Forests provided financial assistance to about 72,000 schools for functioning of Eco-clubs. Each club has 30-50 members taken from the students of Class VI to X. The student members of the Eco-clubs constitute the National Green Corps (NGC). It is proposed to establish Eco-clubs in at least 150 schools in each district of the Country.

The NGC programme addresses various issues concerning protection and improvement of environment, *e.g.*, solid waste management, pollution control, afforestation, maintenance of parks and open spaces, dissemination of information and creation of awareness.

The Government of States and Union Territories have been assigned the responsibility of identifying schools, teachers and nodal agencies. The Nodal Agencies are responsible for implementing, supervising and monitoring the programme. All the States and Union Territories are implementing the programme.

The Government of India provided financial assistance to the State Nodal Agencies for organizing training for Master Trainers and in-charge teacher and for printing and distribution of locally relevant resource material. The Ministry provided a set of resource material in the form of books, posters, booklets, etc., to each Eco-club. Prominent Non-governmental organizations working in the area of environmental education are associated as the Resource Agencies to assist the State Nodal Agencies in implementing the programme. It has also been decided to extend the programme to colleges.

Seminars/Symposia/Workshops/Conferences

Under this programme, financial assistance is provided to educational institutions, non-governmental organizations and others for organizing seminars/symposia/conferences/ workshops on environmental related issues.

Grants in Aid to Professional Societies and Institutions

The major objective of the programme is to provide assistance to professional societies and institutions to augment their capability in the field of environment with an ultimate objective of involving such professional bodies in various activities relating to protection of environment and conservation of natural resources.

Publication of Resources Material

The objective of the programme is to utilise the expertise available with professional societies, voluntary organizations, institutions, etc., for printing and publication of resource material for promoting environmental education and awareness.

Media Action Plan

With the objective of spreading environmental awareness through various media activities, the Government of India has formulated a 'Media Action Plan'. Under the Action Plan, the Ministry of Environment and Forests has taken up several initiatives. These include:

- Launching of a 15 minute programme 'Yeh Gulistan Hamara' in 12 languages on All India Radio.
- A National Theatre Festival on environment was organized.
- A half hour weekly Environmental Magazine Programme on television called BHOOMI, which is being telecast on Doordarshan national channel every sunday.
- To make use of the medium of documentary films for environmental awareness, Memorandum of Under-standing has been signed with Public Service Broadcasting

Trust (PSBT) for production of 13 films every year on environment and their telecast on Doordarshan.

- To take 'Vatavaran' film festival to Indian cities.

The Ministry of Environment and Forests has sponsored 10 lakh 'meghdoot' postcards. These cards carry environmental messages relevant to rural population. Campaigns were planned for using the potential of FM channels effectively. A campaign was launched on various TV channels against the use of firecrackers during festivals. Several features were sponsored on popular magazines such as 'Outlook' and 'Frontline' for highlighting the policies and programmes of the Ministry.

Other Awareness Programmes

(a) *Green Olympiad:* The Ministry of Environment and Forests has sponsored the organization of 'Green Olympiad' (an International Environment Quiz Programme) by The Energy and Resources Institute (TERI). This was conducted in both Hindi and English. More than one lakh school students from India, Russia and UAE participated in this competition. The regional winners were selected for the televised quiz programme named 'TERRAQUIZ', which was telecasted in 13 episodes on the national channel of Doordarshan and it was a great success in sensitising the children about environmental issues.

(b) *National Museum of Natural History:* NMNH was set up to impart non-formal environmental education and conserve the flora, fauna and geological features of the country. This is anchored in various awareness programmes for the student/teacher community as well as for the general public. NMNH and its Regional Museums of Natural History (RMNH) have been able to position in a network of their own to provide dedicated service to the society.

(c) *Workshops:* Teacher orientation workshops on environmental education through 'Low Cost Teaching Aids' and field demonstrations were organized in collaboration with Environmental Planning and Coordination Organization (EPCO).

(d) *Educational Activities:* National Museum of Natural History along with its Regional Museums of Natural History organized several inhouse and outreach programmes for the benefit of children, college students, teachers, challenged children and general public. Various national and international days of scientific relevance like World Wetland Day, Earth Day, Science Day, Conservation Day, World Environment Day and National Environment Awareness Campaign (NEAC) were observed. The museums organized different educational activities and competitions like Quiz, Declamation, On-the-spot Painting, Poster, Essay Writing, Bird Watching, etc., on these occasions.

(e) *Summer Programmes and Nature Camps:* Nature camps were organized as part of the summer and winter vacation programmes for students and teachers. The students were taken to Great Himalayan National Park, Sariska Wildlife Sanctuary, Churdhar Sanctuary and Kanha National Park.

(f) *Collaboration with other Institutions:* The Natural Museum of Natural History and its Regional Museums of Natural History continued their academic and professional collaborations with allied institutions and non-governmental organizations like the National Museum Institute of Museology; Department of Museology, Aligarh Muslim University; Department of Environment, Government of Delhi; Ashoka Trust of Research in Environment and Ecology (ATREE), etc.

(g) *Resource Materials:* The NMNH and its Regional Museums enriched their libraries by addition of good number of books on the subjects of environment and natural history to their existing collections. The NMNH library has more than 15,000 titles of books on environment, natural history, wildlife, ecology, etc., which are in process of retro-conversion into digital format on to a specialized library software. This would enable it to connect to DELNET, the Developing Library Network for better access by users.

Transactional Modalities

A number of the transactional modalities have been suggested by experts across the country and most of them have been included in the National Curriculum Framework 2005. Some of these transactional modalities of Environmental Education are as under: Narration of events, experience and stories, Assignments and projects, Field Trips and Excursion, Formation of Eco-clubs, National Green Corps, Nature Clubs, VIPNET – Clubs , Field Studies and Surveys of the Status of Environmental Resources, Identification of problems and search for solutions, developing strategies for conservation and Awareness Building , Brain Storming and Quizzes, Seminars/Symposia/Workshops, Role Play and Drama, Script-Writing and enactment, Lectures and demonstrations, Discussions, Case-studies and Other Awareness Programmes like Vacation Programmes, Quiz/Essay/Debate/Poster/Slogan competitions, training programmes, etc. This is necessary due to the fact that living conditions of people have become complex due to rapid technological advancements, urbanization and population explosion. These things are desired to be promoted in effective ways through the involvement of school, parents and the community. At secondary level, students need to be introduced to the problems of environment when they live in, the social responsibility of the community in maintaining it, and making it heal.

Teacher and Environmental Awareness

Teacher can play a pivotal role in transmitting knowledge and creating awareness about the environment and help to tackle the local and global environmental issues. The teacher's community should be motivated and committed to the cause of realizing the goals of environmental education and should take initiatives in designing the programme of environmental education. Teachers should be well equipped with the knowledge, method and teaching learning material to inculcate the right understanding and attitude towards environment in the learners.

2. Environmental Attitude

Environmental attitude means to acquire a set of values and feelings of concern for the environment and the motivation of active participation in environmental improvement and protection.

Environmental attitudes are conceptualized in terms of attitude theory as being composed of beliefs and affect towards an object. The environment as an object is difficult to define and this has implications for the study of general environmental attitudes. Attitudes are based on values, have horizontal and vertical structure and tend from general to specific.

Environmental concern appears to be a specific belief which is largely embedded in cognitive structure and should be considered an opinion rather than an attitude. While changes in this opinion have been documented, it is not clear that environmental attitudes or values have shifted, although attitudes have most probably become more differentiated over the last decade. Positive environmental attitudes tend to show consistency with related beliefs and behaviours.

Environmental attitudes are fundamentally important, widely discussed, frequently measured, and poorly understood. In spite of better than 50 years of systematic inquiry into the nature of attitudes by social psychologists, little of this theory has found its way into research on environmental attitudes.

It is observed that degradation of environment mostly occurs due to destruction of natural environments. Now, there is a cry all over for protection and preservation of such natural resources. This can only be possible if we have a right type of attitude towards such issues and if we have proper awareness in the related matters. It is widely accepted that the development of such awareness and attitude can be possible through environmental education. Education is an important social instrument and means, which acts as a catalyst in the improvement of different aspects of life. Knowledge, awareness, skills, values and attitudes acquired through education help one to lead a desired quality of life. In order to protect and conserve the environment enabling people to lead quality life, emphasis need to be given to environmental education in both formal and non-formal system of education. In formal system of education, teaching of environmental education depends not only on curriculum and other facilities provided to the students, but also on the quality of teachers in terms of knowledge, awareness, attitude and skills related to environmental education. Teacher plays a pivotal role in developing desirable attitude towards awareness about environment among students.

Today, the global concern is to struggle against environmental pollution and maintain the standard of human environment. Environment in developing countries like India has been threatened by problems like poverty, pollution and over population. In addition to the industrial revolution, unprecedented scientific and technological revolution has resulted in disastrous changes in the environment leading to environmental degradation/crisis. The speed and nature of environmental change (particularly man-induced change) in recent years have brought about a series of environmental problems of global magnitude – including population explosion, energy resources utilisation, provision of food supplies, exploitation of raw materials and environmental problem (Yashodhara, 2003). This environmental degradation or crisis has become a serious issue as it threatens not only the tranquility of people's existence, but their health and lives as well. As such, the environmental protection and preservation has been an urgent need of the hour. Realizing its importance, the India has also enshrined it into the Constitution, which makes both the state and citizen to 'Protect, preserve and improve the Environment'.

National studies on environmental attitudes are increasingly becoming a part of the environmental policy mix, especially in countries in the North. There are, now, also many cross-cultural surveys. It is notable, however, that such research has mostly been confined to environmental attitudes.

Indian region is particularly an important one for exploring the cultural aspects of environmental attitudes. The various countries in the research have different cultural traditions – and many subcultures – that affect the formation of environmental knowledge, attitudes and behaviour.

Firstly, there is a need for many more subjects than biology and geography to focus on environmental issues. While much work has been done on the environmental dimensions of all subjects in other parts of the world, and on environmental studies and across-the-curriculum approaches to environmental education in primary schools, and teacher education in the Asia-Pacific region, little work has been done to develop an explicit focus on environmental education in secondary schools in India. Students fared much better in understanding traditional concepts from biology and geography than they did in defining the concepts of sustainable development, bio-diversity, carrying capacity, the precautionary principle and intergenerational equity. This requires much greater exposure and discussion than they are receiving at the present time because of their significance in environmental thinking.

Secondly, teachers and students need increased flexibility for choosing topics and issues to investigate so that they may concentrate on the life role relevance of schooling. However, this will require loosening the grip of discipline-based subjects and nationally or centrally determined examinations on the school curriculum. There are enormous barriers to the reorientation of education towards sustainable development, barriers that cannot be addressed by the efforts of individual teachers or even schools, no matter how committed they might be. Effectively addressing barriers such as these requires an appreciation of the role of education in the processes of social continuity and change, the diverse and sometimes contradictory roles of governments, and the corresponding multiple purposes of education.

Thirdly, there is a need for a major philosophical reorientation of school education. Central to this is an understanding of the roles of schooling in social reproduction and the ways in which the structures of school education reproduce, unintentionally perhaps, sustainable development. These structures also provide the context for identifying opportunities and strategies to reorient education towards the development of a civil society based upon the values and practices of sustainability.

Schools serve many purposes today beyond academic ones. Schools are generally public institutions and, in most cases, are subject to the directions of government and its policy-making processes. However, one point seems to be common in all countries. This is that government has multiple and sometimes contradictory roles and these are manifested in diverse ways in educational policies and practices (Carnoy and Levin, 1985; Schlechty, 1990). For example, on one hand, the governments need to ensure that education systems socialise and educate citizens in ways that will enable them to contribute to desired economic activities and goals. This includes vocational knowledge and skills, but also the attitudes of responsibility, diligence, punctuality and social cohesion that will remain and promote these goals. This is the 'reproductive' role of the state and education. On the other hand, the governments, particularly in democratic countries, need to take action to maintain their public legitimacy by anticipating trends that may challenge national well-being and by responding to public concerns about social problems, such as racism, poverty, public safety and, increasingly, the environment. Education is one way in which governments seek to achieve this goal, generally by developing educational policies that enhance the capacities of citizens to respond to anticipated challenges, to identify and articulate their concerns, and to contribute as active and informed citizens to solutions by participating in discussions about them and other public issues. This is the role of the state and education in 'constructing civil society'.

Environmental education has a long history linked with humans growing interaction with the natural environment and developing appropriate attitude towards them. The main objective of environmental education is to develop knowledge based on awareness that will lead to cultivation of responsible attitude to environment, without losing sight of value system of society and individual. Environmental knowledge and awareness would be of no meaning without cultivation of right attitude towards environment, so, attitude is a pre-requisite for fostering valuing approach and responsible action which is an ultimate goal of environmental education.

The relevance of including 'sustainable development' in teacher education syllabi highlights the need for including environmental concerns at all levels of schooling. The Honorable Supreme Court of India has endorsed a model syllabus (2004) prepared by the NCERT for introducing environmental studies as a compulsory subject in the school. With all effort from agencies responsible for determining quality education, school teachers have the major duty to instill values and attitude among students through the subjects they are teaching in school so that students could behave sensibly towards the environment and contribute towards sustainable development. For this noble task, it is necessary that teacher training programme should be designed to equip student teachers, for how to inculcate attitude through different subjects and this requires that student teachers should have positive attitude towards environment to manifest responsible environmental behaviour. Hence, it is pertinent to assess the attitude of the students of teacher training programme. The environmental threats in India include the degradation of rural land to the pollution, rapid urbanization with encroachment of forests, accommodating fast growing population and increasing congested cities. The plight is that the industrialization is the demand of the day where the nation has not yet arrived with a mechanism of conserving the environment and protecting it from the hazards caused due to constant effort of tshe country for modern amenities and making it 'livable' for civil society. The world is now alarmed with various environmental problems, such as climate change, ozone layer depletion, global warming, and so on. Many of these problems are the result of irresponsible environmental behaviour, which is highly influenced by the attitudes that the people possess. In other words, people's decision making is also guided by the values and attitudes they possess. Environmental attitude is therefore a big concern in significant environmental education research. Young people will be affected and there is a need to provide solutions to environmental problems that resulted as a result of present-day actions. Consequently, promoting environmental attitude has been considered as important. Environmental attitude is fundamentally important, widely discussed, frequently measured, and poorly understood.

3. Environmental Ethics

The whole world's attention is now focused on the state of environment degradation brought about by developments in science and technology and the need to satisfy the demands of the growing population. Every human being has the right of decent life, but today there are elements in our environment that tend to militate against the attainment and enjoyment of such a life. The exacerbation of the pollution of environment can cause untold misery. Unhappiness and suffering to human beings crop up, simply because of our lack of concern for the common good and the absence of sense of responsibility and ethics for sustaining a balanced eco-system. If we are to aspire to a better quality of life, one which will ensure freedom from want, from disease and from fear itself, then we must all join hands to stem the increasing toxification of this earth.

Environmental ethics studies the ethical relationship between human beings and the environment. Plants and animals are an integral part of the environment and hence have a right to be considered a part of the human life; they should also be associated with our guiding principles as well as our moral and ethical values. Unfortunately, they are often ignored during talks about the philosophical principle that guides our life. Most of the human activities lead to environmental pollution disturbing the balance in the nature depriving all the life forms of their right to live. Environmental ethics says that we should base our behaviour on a set of ethical values that guide our approach towards the other living beings in nature. The conservation of natural resources is not only the need of the day but also our prime duty. Environmental ethics has given a new dimension to the conservation of natural resources.

Environmental ethics has been regarded as an important component of environmental education. Environmental education aims at not only providing information about environmental issues but also enabling people to think, judge, choose environmentally responsible behaviours that is considered important for the development of education. It is the discipline that studies the moral relationship of human beings and also the value and moral status of the environment and its non-human contents.

The constitution of India explicitly makes environmental conservation a duty. The Government of India and all constitutional states within India now have a Ministry or Department of Environment. Education Ministries and Departments recognise environmental education as an essential part of education. The law courts of the country have been sympathetic to environmental causes. India has a very large number of active NGOs that are involved in a variety of activities from policy analysis to school programmes, from participatory natural resources management to activism.

There are many challenges for environmental educators in India. Some of them are:

1. The challenge, in a large and diverse country, is to find out the right blend between centralized and de-centralized efforts and approaches.
2. The challenge of reaching out to large numbers cost effectively.
3. The challenge of making environmental considerations relevant and meaningful to various groups.
4. The challenge of putting environmental education on the agenda of educational decision-makers.
5. The challenge of putting sustainable development concerns high on the agenda of policy-makers.

6. Finding and developing human and financial resources for environmental education.

The National Policy on Education (1986) of India states that protection of environment is a value which, along with certain other values, must form an integral part of the curriculum at all stages of education.

Principles of Environmental Ethics

Three normative principles of environmental ethics are:

1. *Principles of Environmental Justice:* Environmental justice is the minimum ethical stance of environmental ethics. There are two dimensions to environmental justice. Distributive environmental justice concerns the equal distribution of environmental benefits and burdens, whereas participatory environmental justice focuses on opportunities to participate in decision-making. While domestic environmental justice is easily understood and accepted, the institutionalizing of global environmental justice remains a challenge to global society. The seventeen principles of environmental justice issued at the First National People of Colour Environmental Leadership Summit in 1991 is a good starting point for environmental ethics.
2. *Principle of Intergenerational Equality:* The principle of intergenerational equality is an extension of that of equality. Equal rights constitute the core of the principle of equality. The rights to life, liberty and happiness are basic human rights shared by everyone, future generations as well as the present generation. Every generation should leave the following generation an equal opportunity to live a happy life. Thus, it is the duty of any given generation to bequeath to their descendants not only a just politico-economic system, but also a healthy and generative earth.
3. *Principle of Respect for Nature:* Though they may come from different perspectives, most environmental ethicists agree that we have a duty to conserve and protect the integrity of the eco-system and its bio-diversity. No one doubts that the prosperity of human beings depends on the

prosperity of nature. Human beings are part of nature, and the human economy is a sub-system of nature's economy; the former must fit into the latter and abide by the laws of the latter. Earth is the planet that is our home. This home planet is in crisis now. We must carry out our duty, therefore, to care for it.

If we want to secure the future of our environment, we have to create awareness and ethics about environment and an attitude of caring and sharing of natural resources in the mind of those who are the future of our nation. As rightly said by Pandit Jawaharlal Nehru, the former Prime Minister of India, that the future of India in shaped in her classrooms, where teacher is the central figure. So, we can say that the key of successful environmental education is the teacher. The teacher plays an important role in shaping and molding the habits, manners and good character of the children. Therefore, to gear up the environmental education programme, it is essential that teacher should have sufficient knowledge of environmental education.

Quality environmental education in school depends more on the qualification, teaching experience and preparation of teachers than it does on school curricula. If teachers do not have the awareness, skills, commitment, ethics, values and an attitude to environmentalise their curriculum, it is unlikely that environmentally literate students will be produced. Unfortunately, there is dearth of teachers and teacher educators to handle environmental problems as they lack awareness, ethics expertise and perfect training in environmental education.

Education for Environmental Ethics

Overcoming global environmental crisis depends ultimately on how humankind's values, attitudes and behaviours change. Education is critical for the structural transformation of industrial society. UNESCO plays a key role in encouraging Member States, especially developing countries, to advance environmental education and to incorporate environmental ethics into their educational systems.

1. *Formulating A Syllabus of Environmental Ethics:* To lead and direct the teaching of environmental ethics, UNESCO could formulate a flexible syllabus of environmental ethics for undergraduates, recommending two or three textbooks and encouraging member states to translate them into their native languages.
2. *Co-operating with Education Services of Member States:* Education officers must recognise the importance of values and engage in promoting environmental ethics. To promote the teaching of environmental ethics, UNESCO should establish a stable mechanism of dialogue and information-sharing among the education sectors of its Member States.
3. *Training Teachers in Environmental Ethics:* Environmental education teachers bear a responsibility to propagate the ideas of environmental ethics. It is extremely important to deepen their understanding of environmental issues and to improve their skills in teaching environmental ethics. Those who are able to profit from advanced training classes should commit to offering environmental ethics classes at their universities under UNESCO supervision.

The effective Environmental Education teacher should be able to ...

1. Apply knowledge of educational philosophy to the selection and development of curricular programmes and strategies to achieve both general education and E.E. goals. (It is important that all educators be aware of the philosophical basis for education in their own society. Environmental education goals and methods should be evaluated in the light of such philosophies as Experimentalism (Dewey) or Reconstructionism (Brammel). Many accepted goals of general education supported by such philosophies are entirely consistent with E.E. goals. General education materials and methods may sometimes need to be merely 'environmentalized' to achieve the goals).

2. Utilise current theories of moral reasoning in selecting, developing and/or implementing E.E. curricula which will effectively achieve accepted goals of E.E. with selected receiver groups. (Included in this category of 'moral reasoning' are not only theories of moral development such as Kohlberg's, but theories of valuing processes as well. E.E. teachers should be competent to assess the developmental readiness of receivers when dealing with attitudes and processes in the affective domain, and to utilise appropriate strategies to allow receivers to recognise the role of values in environmental decision making, clarify value positions, and understand the valuing process.)
3. Utilise current theories of knowledge/attitude/behaviour relationships in selecting, developing and/or implementing a balanced curriculum which maximizes the probability of desired behaviour changes in receivers. (Environmental educators often assume linear relationships among ecological knowledge, positive environmental attitudes, and environmentally ethical behaviour. Current research in the field indicates that such may not be the case. E.E. teachers must balance their curriculum in view of the roles of various categories of knowledge (*e.g.*, ecological knowledge *vs.* trade-off costs), experiences, and locus of control (internal or external) in leading to desired behavioural outcomes.)
4. Utilise current theories of learning (*e.g.*, Piaget, Bruner, Gagne) in selecting, developing, and/or implementing curricular materials and teaching strategies to effectively achieve E.E. goals with selected receiver groups. (The nature of many E.E. goals is problem solving. Learning theory has much to offer in guiding the selection of materials, and strategies for specific receiver age levels may be effective when theories of learning development (*e.g.*, Piaget) are considered. A pragmatic approach to this body of knowledge would do much to increase the effectiveness of E.E. teachers.)

5. Apply the theory of transfer of learning in selecting, developing or implementing curricular materials and strategies to ensure that learned knowledge, attitudes, and cognitive skills will be transferred to life style decision-making by receivers. (The ultimate goal of E.E. is to produce environmentally literate citizens who are willing and capable of taking positive environmental actions in their lives. Too often, educators fail to teach for the transfer of knowledge, attitudes and cognitive processes by receivers for use both within and outside the formal classroom.)
6. Select effective instructional methodologies which are appropriate for desired cognitive and affective outcomes, receiver characteristics, and available facilities (*e.g.*, time, money, personnel).
7. Effectively implement the following methodologies to achieve E.E. goals:
   - *(a)* Outdoor education methods;
   - *(b)* Affective education methods (*e.g.*, values clarification, Bank's inquiry model, moral dilemma model);
   - *(c)* Simulation games (including role playing);
   - *(d)* Case study methods;
   - *(e)* Community resource use (ecological, issue-related, human resources);
   - *(f)* Methods of autonomous student and/or group investigation, evaluation and action planning for resolving environmental issues; and
   - *(g)* Appropriate teacher behaviour while handling controversial environmental issues.
8. Develop and use effective means of planning for instruction.
9. Effectively infuse of appropriate E.E. curricula and methods into all disciplines to which the teacher is assigned.
10. Effectively evaluate E.E. curricula and methods of achievement with receivers in both cognitive and affective domains.

Competencies in Environmental Education Content

Level I: Ecological Foundations

The effective E.E. teacher should be able to ...

11. Apply knowledge of ecological foundations to the analysis of environmental issues and identify key ecological principles involved.
12. Apply knowledge of ecological foundations to predict the ecological consequences of alternative solutions to environmental problems.
13. Be sufficiently literate in ecology to identify, select, and interpret appropriate sources of scientific information in a continuing effort to investigate, evaluate and find solutions for environmental problems.
14. Communicate and apply in an educational context, the major concepts in ecology.

Level II: Conceptual Awareness

The effective E.E. teacher should be able to select, develop and/or implement curricular materials which will effectively make receivers aware of...

15. How man's cultural activities (*e.g.*, religious, economic, political, social, etc.) influence the environment from an ecological perspective?
16. How individual behaviour shows impact on the environment from an ecological perspective?
17. A wide variety of local, regional, national and international environmental issues and the ecological and cultural implications of these issues.
18. The viable alternative solutions available for remediating discrete environmental issues and the ecological and cultural implications of these alternative solutions.
19. The need for environmental issue investigation and evaluation as a prerequisite to sound decision-making.
20. The roles played by differing human values in environmental issues and the need for personal values clarification as an integral part of environmental decision-making.

21. The need for responsible citizenship action (*e.g.*, persuasion, consumerism, legal action, political action, ecomanagement) in the remediation of environmental issues.

Level III: Investigation and Evaluation

The effective E.E. teacher should be competent to investigate environmental issues and evaluate alternative solutions and to develop, select and/or implement curricular materials and strategies which will develop similar competencies in receivers, including ...

22. The knowledge and skills needed to identify and investigate issues (using both primary and seondary sources of information and to synthesize the data gathered).
23. The ability to analyze environmental issues and the associated value perspectives with respect to their ecological and cultural implications.
24. The ability to identify alternative solutions for discrete issues and the value perspectives associated with these solutions.
25. The ability to autonomously evaluate alternative solutions and associated value perspectives for discrete environmental issues with respect to their cultural and ecological implications.
26. The ability to identify and clarify their own value positions related to discrete environmental issues and their associated solutions.
27. The ability to evaluate, clarify, and change their own value positions in the light of new information.

Level IV: Environmental Action Skills

The effective E.E. teacher should be competent to take positive environmental action for the purpose of achieving and/or maintaining a dynamic equilibrium between quality of life and the quality of environment, and to develop, select, and/or implement curricular materials and strategies to develop similar competencies in receivers to take individual or group action when appropriate.

Environmental Literacy is a conceptual learning to develop people knowing in terms of environmental education. It is, beyond the term environmental literacy as a certain cognitive skills and basic definition, claimed that environmental literacy builds on an ecological paradigm. Environmental literacy is the capacity to perceive and interpret the relative health of environmental systems and to take appropriate action to maintain, restore, or improve the health of those systems.

Teachers can provide a vital link in the delivery of environmental knowledge, its associated problems and their solutions. Environmental education must utilise diverse learning environments and a broad array of educational approaches to teaching and learning and stress practical activities and first hand experiences. Environmental education should be a continues lifelong experience, beginning at the preschool stage continuing through all formal and non-formal stages and should be interdisciplinary discipline in making possible a holistic and balanced perspective.

The universities and educational institutions have designed the course content of environmental education for B.Ed. and M.Ed. courses. The main emphasis has been given on physical and biological component of the environment. The teaching methodology of physical sciences, bioscience and social sciences are taught and practiced under the main course of teacher education. Therefore, the related concepts and components of environment can be easily included in these teaching subjects of teacher education curriculum. The main aim of the environmental education is to develop constructive attitude towards the environment, to develop awareness of and concern about the environment and its associated problems and to understand about the complex nature of environment. It offers an effective instrument for embedding in them the desirable environmental ethics. So, keeping all these aim in mind, environmental education teacher should prepare well himself for teaching.

STATEMENT OF THE PROBLEM

A Study of Environmental Awareness, Environmental Attitude and Environmental Ethics of Teacher Education Students.

NEED OF THE STUDY

Today, qualitative improvement of education is of great importance and it can be achieved only by improving the quality of instruction. Even though great advancement in science as well as in educational technology are made everywhere in the world, the methods of teaching prevalent now-a-days are not significant to meet the requirements of students of different levels. Several studies on classroom practices reveal that even though the student characteristics and societal expectations have changed, our educators still employ traditional methods and modes of instruction. To train reflective and totally active world of citizens, many of our traditional educational practices must be seriously questioned and novel approaches based on sound objectives must be implemented. Hence, it is necessary to refine and improve the teaching methods and instructional techniques to realize the fullest potentialities of individual learners.

Education, for all its remarkable achievements, still is largely unable to accommodate individual student learning needs and to achieve acceptable levels of individual student mastery, proficiency and expertise.

Even though the academic community, including curriculum planners, educationalists and teachers are quite aware of the need for the development of environmental awareness at every level, it has been neglected till recently in our educational system. Unfortunately, our present method of teaching environmental science is based on giving information as bit and/by bit. It demands rote memorization of concepts, facts and principles and, through this traditional methods of teaching, the objectives of environmental education are not realized. Therefore, we are in need of new strategies for developing environmental awareness which help to accomplish definite goals. To develop environmental awareness among teacher education students, we must rely on systematic and effective instructional strategies.

The key to successful environmental education is the classroom teacher. If teacher does not possess knowledge, skill and commitment to environmentalise their curriculum, it is unlikely that an environmentally literate student will be produced. For this, special training to prospective teachers is necessary. There is a need for a new personal and indivudualized behaviour based on global ethics, which can be realized only through the enlightenment and training of educational professionals. The teacher should be aware of the environmental education aspects, only then he can make the future generation aware of the environmental problems and their solutions. Taking into consideration this situation, the investigator felt a need to conduct a study to know about the environmental attitude possessed by student teachers so that necessary actions could be taken up to come forward with prolific result for enhancing the efficiency of the content provided to them as well as to sustain their inner urge for desirable actions.

There is importance of the formal teaching of environmental ethics because environmental ethics is needed to respond to the environmental issues generated. Environmental concerns will always be a controversial aspect of society. Educators have a responsibility to provide information about human health concerns, habitat relationships, development, earth resources, etc., and their relationship to political and personal decision making and laws. Generally, educators promote the ethics and values that have general societal consensus, but students will enter the process with their own judgements and ideas regarding environment.

Although most of this research does not distinguish between provision within primary or secondary teacher training courses, evidence can be found to suggest that the greatest inadequacies that occur in the training of the school teacher. These courses place more emphasis on providing environmental information, especially about the natural environment, rather than considering environmental education approaches and methodologies. Furthermore, they stress the cognitive elements at the expense of the affective components of environmental education. The lack of attention to environmental education in teacher education is a serious problem where basic education is the key priority. The importance of the primary years of schooling in the education of the child has been grossly under-estimated.

The lack of appropriate teacher training courses within the field is of great significance to environmental education. Attitudes towards the environment are generally acquired very early in life and the early years of schooling are formative ones for development of environmental attitudes. Learning of attitudes and values are so important for imaginative action in environmental issues which are vital and needs to be considered carefully early in these sequences of life long learning. Thus, the need to correct the existing situation within teacher education courses is crucial to the future of environmental education.

SCOPE OF THE STUDY

The present study was intended to measure the environmental awareness, environmental attitude and environmental ethics of teacher education students.

The present study is limited to the variables, *viz.*, male versus female teacher education students, rural versus urban teacher education students, science versus arts teacher education students, government versus private college teacher education students, teacher education students with teaching experience versus without teaching experience, teacher education students, aged below 25 years and above 25 years, and B.Ed. *vs.* M.Ed. teacher education students. The present study is confined to teacher education students of Hyderabad and secunderabad and their surrounding rural areas.

OBJECTIVES OF THE STUDY

The objectives of the present study entitled "A study of Environmental Awareness, Environmental Attitude and Environmental Ethics of Teacher Education Students" are:

1. To find out the environmental awareness, environmental attitude and environmental ethics of teacher education students.
2. To find out the difference in the environmental awareness, environmental attitude and environmental ethics of male and female teacher education students.
3. To find out the difference in the environmental awareness, environmental attitude and environmental ethics of rural and urban teacher education students.
4. To find out the difference in the environmental awareness, environmental attitude and environmental ethics of science and arts teacher education students.
5. To find out the difference in the environmental awareness, environmental attitude and environmental ethics of government and private college teacher education students.
6. To find out the difference in the environmental awareness, environmental attitude and environmental ethics of teacher education students with teaching experience and without teaching experience.
7. To find out the difference in the environmental awareness, environmental attitude and environmental ethics of teacher education students aged below 25 years and above 25 years.
8. To find out the difference in the environmental awareness, environmental attitude and environmental ethics of B.Ed. and M.Ed. teacher education students.
9. To find out the association among environmental awareness, environmental attitude and environmental ethics of teacher education students.
10. To find out the association among environmental awareness, environmental attitude and environmental ethics of male and female teacher education students, rural and urban teacher education students, science and arts teacher education students, government and private college teacher education students, teacher education

students with and without teaching experience, teacher education students aged below 25 years and above 25 years, and B.Ed. and M.Ed. teacher education students.

This study is undertaken to study the level of environmental awareness, environmental attitude and environmental ethics of teacher education students and association among environmental awareness, environmental attitude and environmental ethics of teacher education students.

EDUCATIONAL IMPLICATIONS OF THE STUDY

It is responsibility of teacher training institutions to develop environmental awareness, environmental attitude and environmental ethics in student teachers. For this purpose, environmental education should be made compulsory in teacher education programmes.

Education about the environment as it is concerned with the knowledge of environment.

Education for the environment is concerned with attitude and values for the environment.

Education through the environment using the environment as a resource for learning based on the philosophy of either infusion into the existing curricula or insertion of new course of study.

It is the also responsibility of the institutions such as NCERT, SCERT, NIEPA, Academic staff colleges and Departments of Education in the Universities to promote environmental awareness and develop environmental ethics in in-service teachers and teacher educators desirable for environmental conservation.

All these can be achieved, if the environmental awareness, environmental attitude and environmental ethics are assessed. Hence, is the present study.

2

REVIEW OF RELATED LITERATURE

The review of related literature provides a comprehensive understanding about what has already been known about a topic. It forms the basis for subscribing rationale for having chosen the problem for the study. Review of related literature allows the researcher to acquaint him (her) self with the current knowledge in the field or area in which he/she is going to conduct his/her research. It enables the researcher to define the limits of his/her study. It also helps the researcher to delimit and define his/her problem. The knowledge of the related literature brings the researcher up-to-date on the work, which others have done and thus state the objectives clearly and concisely.

By reviewing the related literature, the researcher can avoid unfruitful and useless problem areas. The researcher can select those areas in which positive findings are very likely to result and his endeavours are likely to add to the knowledge in a meaningful way. Through the review of related literature, the researcher can avoid unintentional duplication of well established facts. It is of no use to replicate a study when the stability and validity of its results have been clearly established.

The review of related literature gives the researcher an understanding of the research methodology, which refers to the way the study is to be conducted. It helps the researcher to know about the tools and instruments, which proved to be useful and promising in the previous studies. It also provides an insight into the statistical methods, through which the validity of the results is to be established.

Good, Barr and Scates (1941) analysed the purpose of review of related literature as: "To show whether the available evidence material solves the problem adequately without further investigation; To provide ideas, theories, explanations or hypotheses valuable in formulating the present study; To suggest the research methods to the problems; To locate comparative data useful in interpretation of the results; To contribute to the general scholarship of the investigator. It helps the research worker to find out what is already known, what others have attempted to find out, what methods of attack have been promising or disappointing and what problems remain to be solved; It furnishes him with indispensable suggestions about comparative data, good procedures, likely methods and tried techniques; It makes him alert to research possibilities that have been over looked and research approaches that have proved to be sterile; and It prevents pointless repetition of research".

The important specific reason for reviewing the related literature is to know about the recommendations of the previous researchers, listed in their studies for further research.

From the above discussion, it seems clean clear that for any worthwhile investigation, a review of literature in the concerned field is of great help to the investigator. The studies tell us how much work has been already done in a certain field and provide necessary knowledge and insight into the methods used to collect, analyse and interpret data and findings. It also suggests solutions and recommendations. Having realized the importance of related studies, the investigator tried to study and record the related literature.

In the review of related literature, the findings of the research studies are quoted as under:

1. Studies related to Environmental Awareness.

2. Studies related to Environmental Attitude.
3. Studies related to Environmental Ethics.
4. Studies related to the association among Environmental Awareness, Environmental Attitude and Environmental Ethics.

ENVIRONMENTAL AWARENESS

The findings of the previous research related to environmental awareness are presented here under.

Environmental Awareness and Teachers

Halverson (1982) suggested that special training and commitment are necessary to bring the outlook within education which prospective teachers may not have experienced in their own education.

Jayanti and Parama (1983) suggested that environmental education in secondary stage of study should be adopted depending on the infrastructural facilities and availability of trained teachers.

Mishra, *et.al.* (1985) have highlighted the vital role of teacher education in equiping teachers to teach environmental education effectively.

Simpson, *et.al.* (1988) stated that intensive teacher education was not merely a orientation but a thorough change in both outlook and preparation of teachers and teacher educators.

UNESCO – UNEP (1990) highlighted the role of teacher education in environmental improvement reflecting a growing international and intergovernmental recognition of the need to train teachers in the field.

Shahnawaj (1990) found that the teachers had more environmental awareness than students.

Prahara (1991) observed a low level of environmental awareness among preservice teachers.

Patel and Patel (1995) noticed a significant impact of environmental awareness of teachers.

Seeni and Manickam (2002) found that awareness about environmental education was created with the help of teachers and NGOs.

Nagaraja Rao (2004) noticed that students' effective interaction with environment was motivated and guided by the teacher.

Sahaya Mary and Paul Raj (2005) found that the teacher trainees had significant difference in terms of age.

Bela Yavetz and Daphne Goldman (2009) observed that the decision makers bring environmental education into the policy of teacher education institutions and for programme developers on effective direction for integrating environmental education giving structures and frameworks of current programme.

Tahsin Khalid (2010) found that many pre-service high school teachers possessed an array of misconceptions about the causes and effects of green house effect, ozone depletion and acid rain.

Liesje Coertjens and Jelle Boeve Pauw (2010) found that the schools in which science was taught in a more hands on manner were associated with higher student environmental awareness.

Vipinder Nagra (2010) observed a significant variation in the environmental education awareness level of school teachers in relation to their level and subject specialization.

Harjeet Kaur (2012) found that students showed more environmental awareness after studying the subject of environmental education at under graduate level.

Amritpal Kaur and Mahabir Singh (2012) stated the importance of environmental education in teacher education where the teachers should be well equipped with the knowledge, method and teaching learning material to inculcate the right understanding of environmental awareness and develop attitude towards environment in learners.

Environmental Awareness and Teacher Education Students

Abayomi Serifi (1981) found that pre-service and in-service teachers had very little knowledge of environmental action skill, and made little use of defined criteria in implementing environmental action.

Shahnawaj (1990) found that trained and untrained teachers didn't differ on environmental awareness.

Pradhan (1995) revealed that teacher trainees having master's degree and belonging to science group had significantly higher environmental awareness than all the other groups of subjects.

Lane, *et.al.* (1995) suggested that preparation in environmental education teaching methods contributes to teacher's perceived competencies in teaching about environment.

Wade (1996) argued that the environmental education needs to re-evaluate its approach to teacher education.

Smith and Smith (1997) indicated that teachers having more preservice and in-service training have largely positive attitudes, but do not spend much time in teaching about environment or environmental issues.

Seema, Rawat and Veena (1997) observed that student teachers before training had less environmental awareness as compared to post training.

Wai Kevin (1999) found that teacher trainees received a modest score in their environmental awareness and environmental disposition assessment.

Shobeiri, Omidar and Prahallada (2007) observed a significant difference in Indian and Iranian student teachers in their environmental awareness.

Astalin (2008) found that general category student teachers had higher environmental awareness than SC and OBC candidates and found no significant difference between SC and OBC student teachers.

Bela Yavetz and Daphne Goldman (2009) observed a low level of environmental awareness among prospective teachers.

Sara Peer and Daphne Goldman (2010) found that the student teachers of Israel had limited environmental knowledge and awareness.

Tali Tal (2010) noticed that the pre-service students after taking introductory environmental education course increased their environmental knowledge acquisition as well as their environmental awareness. These students were reflected a variety of teaching methods and especially on the online debate forum and on field trips.

Ajay Kumar (2010) found that environmental awareness of prospective teachers of Himachal Pradesh remains almost same due to the fact that they were studying Education for Human Value, Environment and Human Rights as compulsory subject during their B.Ed. course.

Mustafa Metin, Kerem Coskun and Yavuz Topkaya (2011) observed that Turkish pre-service teachers did not have enough environmental awareness though Education Primary Behaviouristic Approach in curriculum was used to educate them.

Manpreet Kaur (2012) found that B.Ed. students of Patiala possessed an adequate level of environmental awareness.

Environmental Awareness and Gender

Abayomi Serifi (1981) found that male in-service teachers were possessing significantly higher environmental awareness than female inservice teachers.

Magheda (1985) noticed gender differences among Kenyan students regarding environmental issues.

Shahnawaj (1990) found that the girls possessed significantly more awareness about the environment than boys.

Paramjeet (1993) observed that environmental awareness was more among boys of better socio-economic status; where as among girls, it was observed that the girls of lower socio-economic status had more environmental awareness as compared to boys.

Patel (1995) observed that the D.Ed. girl students were more sensitive to environmental issues than D.Ed. boys.

Tripathi (2000) found that boys had better awareness than girls.

Jyotsna (2003) found gender difference in the environmental awareness.

Sebastian and Nima (2005) informed that the boys, especially from urban areas, had more environmental awareness than girls.

Abraham and Arjunan (2005) found that boys had more environmental awareness than girls.

Pareer (2006) found a significant difference in the environmental awareness between male and female students.

Nagra and Dhillon (2006) found that male student teachers had more environmental awareness than female teacher students.

Shobeiri, Omidvar and Prahallada (2007) observed more environmental awareness in boys than girls.

Mustafa (2008) found that female elementary teacher education students who had less than three brothers and sisters with high socio-economic level had more environmental awareness.

Astalin (2008) found a significant difference in environmental awareness in male and female student teachers.

Rao (2010) found that male and female D.Ed. students had equal environmental awareness.

Pushpa Latha (2010) observed no significant difference between environmental awareness of male and female B.Ed. student teachers.

Vipinder Nagra (2010) observed no significant difference in environmental awareness of male and female B.Ed. student teachers.

Donald E. Riechard and Sandra J. Peterson (2010) noticed that female student teachers had significantly higher perception of risk scores of environmental awareness than male student teachers.

Saheblal Mahiboob Nadaf (2011) found that B.Ed. male teacher trainees with extroversion/introversion personality factor, lower/higher self-concept and lower/higher study habits do not differ significantly in respect to their proneness to environmental awareness.

Bhim Chandra Mondal (2011) observed no significant difference in environmental awareness of male and female B.Ed. student teachers.

Manpreet Kaur (2012) found that male student teachers had less environmental awareness than female teacher students.

Environmental Awareness and Locality

Rajput, Gupta and Grewal (1981) found that school going rural children had better than urban students with regard to environmental awareness.

Gupta (1981) found a significant difference between school-going rural children and school-going urban children in environmental awareness and school-going rural children had more environmental awareness.

Pradhan (1995) found a significant difference in the environmental awareness between rural and urban teacher trainees; the urban teacher trainees had more environmental awareness.

Sabhlok (1995) found that urban teachers differed significantly from rural and tribal teachers on their awareness of environmental problems.

Dinakara (2000) reported a significant difference in environmental awareness between urban and rural school teachers.

Durga Malathi (2002) found a significant difference between rural and urban students in their environmental awareness.

Jalan Somanathan and Saraswatha Chaudhri (2003) noticed a significant difference in environmental awareness in rural and urban students.

Pareer (2005) found a significant difference between rural and urban students in their environmental awareness.

William Dharma Raja, *et.al.* (2005) noticed that the prospective teachers from rural and urban areas had very high awareness of environment, yet they do not put it into practice.

Abraham and Arjunan (2005) found that urban senior secondary students had more environmental awareness than rural students.

Nagra and Dhillon (2006) found that urban school teachers had high environmental awareness than rural teachers.

Shobeiri, Omidvar and Prahallada (2007) found that urban student teachers had more environmental awareness than rural student teachers.

Astalin (2008) found that urban scores for male students was higher than girls and rural scores for boys was not significant than girls.

Pushap Latha (2010) found that B.Ed. student teachers belonging to urban areas had more environmental awareness in comparison with rural B.Ed. student teachers.

Ajay Kumar (2010) observed no significant difference in environmental awareness of rural and urban prospective teachers.

Rao (2010) found that D.Ed. students belonging to urban areas had more environmental awareness in comparison with rural D.Ed. students.

Bhim Chandra (2011) noticed that B.Ed. student teachers belonging to urban areas had more environmental awareness in comparison with rural B.Ed. student teachers.

Mageswamy Karpudewan (2011) found a low level of environmental awareness in urban students.

Environmental Awareness and Course Subjects

Bhattacharya (1977) found that students of science had more environmental awareness than the students of non-science subjects.

Pradhan (1995) revealed that the subject background of the trainees had its effect on the knowledge and understanding of facts and concepts relating to different aspects of environmental problems.

Shabina (1999) observed that science teachers were rated high when compared to arts teachers.

Badkobi and Hadipour (2001) found that science teachers had high environmental awareness compared to arts teachers.

Shaila (2003) found that the secondary school science teachers had high environmental awareness compared to arts teachers.

Vipender and Jaswinder (2003) noticed that science teachers had more environmental awareness than arts teachers.

Vipinder Nagra (2010) observed no significant difference between environmental awareness of arts and science B.Ed. student teachers.

Pushpa Latha (2010) noticed an equal environmental awareness in arts and science B.Ed. student teachers.

Ajay Kumar (2010) observed no significant difference in arts and science prospective teachers.

Harjeet Kaur (2012) noticed no significant difference in prospective arts and science teachers.

Environmental Awareness and Management of the Institution

Balamurugan (2005) study showed a significant difference in environmental awareness and school types.

Anna Uitto and Kalle Juuti (2011) found that schools' own environmental projects and participation in programmes were linked to environmental awareness and enhanced student's interest in environmental issues.

Environmental Awareness and Curriculum

Pai (1981) found a significant difference in the performance of the experimental group compared with the control group. The performance of the students in the experimental group showed that they had gained an overall knowledge in environmental problems as a result of instructions for using curriculum.

Mishra, *et.al.* (1985) anticipated the development of an effective teacher training course in environmental education would result in a top-down curriculum innovation approach.

Fullan and Stiegelbauer (1991) suggested for the preparation and adoption of new curriculum guidelines, syllabuses, teaching activities, use of new forms of pedagogy and assessment and the reflective development of teacher's beliefs or practical theories of education.

Fien and Tilbury (1996) developed a multimedia teacher education programme for adding effective changes to classroom practice. This included reforms to curriculum and pedagogy, which can help empower teachers to take responsibility for planning learning experiences.

Ramakrishna (2003) suggested that the children should be exposed to environmental activities similar to curricular activities.

Sharma (2003) indicated that, although environmental education was taken up as a subject in the curriculum, the subject faces certain limitations with regard to its proper implementation.

Mageswamy (2011) found that green chemistry curriculum constituted a suitable context for supporting pre-service teachers in their development of pro-environmental attitudes.

Harjeet Kaur (2012) found that students showed more environmental awareness after studying the subject of environmental education, as their post-test scores on environmental awareness questionnaire was higher than pre-test scores.

Environmental Awareness and Teacher Education Students

Rajput, Saxena and Jadhao (1980) made an attempt to identify the awareness of children of primary level towards the scientific and social environment where they found experimental groups were significantly better than the control groups.

Anthony Swamy (1990) found that the school dropouts taught by video method learned more concepts on environment than those who were taught by using charts.

Kidwai Zeerat (1991) developed a framework for an environment – oriented geography curriculum to secondary stage students.

Gopala Krishna and Sarojini (1992) suggested that the participatory learning approach could bring about a better impact with regard to environmental awareness.

Gnanadevan (2007) noticed that the environmental awareness of higher secondary students was high.

Chandrasekhar (2008) concluded that environmental awareness of high school students was moderate.

Harjeet Kaur (2012) stated that students showed more environmental awareness after studying the subject of environmental education.

ENVIRONMENTAL ATTITUDE

The findings of the previous research related to environmental attitude are presented here under.

Environmental Attitude and In-service and Pre-service Teachers

Stuart William (1979) found that the traditional or teacher-directed courses in environmental science were more likely to change the environmental attitudes and knowledge of student teachers.

Robert (1988) revealed that the environmental attitude of student teachers could be modified for inculcating positive attitude towards environment and to manifest responsible environmental behaviour.

Shahnawaj (1990) found that 95 per cent teachers and 94 per cent students possessed positive environmental attitudes. Trained teachers in environmental education did not differ in their environmental attitude.

Prahara (1991) found a moderate environmental attitude in inservice teachers.

Seema and Veena (1997) revealed that the student teachers before training had less environmental attitude as compared to the post training.

Leming, *et.al.* (1997) found that classes participating in pro-environmental activities showed positive effect towards student attitude regarding environment.

Chung (1999) found a positive attitude of teacher trainees towards environmental protection, yet their behaviour and habit were not entirely consistent to the stated attitudes.

Shaila (2003) found no difference with gender in the environmental attitude of secondary school teachers.

Larijani and Yeshodhara (2006) found that Iranian prospective teachers had most favourable attitude in all the components except in wild life.

Shobeiri, *et.al.* (2006) noticed a significant difference between Indian and Iranian primary school teachers in their level of environmental attitude.

Kumar and Patil (2007) found that students with environmental education background had better environmental attitude.

Kumar, Mangala and Patil (2007) found that environmental education background helped to have better environmental attitude.

Maryam, Larijani and Yeshodhara (2008) found that Iranian teachers had more positive environmental attitude than Indian teachers.

Tuncer and Tekkaya (2009) observed that environmental background of pre-service teachers was positively related to environmental literacy and attitudes along with other uses affected significantly by gender.

Ogunbiyi (2009) observed no significant main effect of treatment on pre-service teachers' knowledge of environmental concepts and attitude towards environment.

Bela Yavetz (2009) found that environmental attitude was positive both at the beginning and end of the study on environmental behaviour.

Sara Peer and Daphne Goldman (2010) found that Israeli student teachers had a positive attitude towards environment.

Liesje Coertjens and Jelle Boeve de Pauw (2010) found that environmental learning activities were associated with more pro-environmental attitude among student teachers.

Cheong (2010) found that training of pre-service teachers related to community problems and the reflections about what they had learnt in being involved with the projects show the capacity building efforts possible to work towards sustainable development and the development of knowledge, skills and attitudes.

Sudeshana (2010) observed a significant difference for both environmental attitude and responsible environmental behaviour between in-service and pre-service teachers.

Anna Uitto and Kalle Juuti (2011) observed a significant correlation between environmental attitude and environmental factors.

Gulderen Saglam (2011) stated that English language pre-service teachers had relatively increased mildly positive environmental attitude.

Mahbub Sarkar (2011) found that students had favourable environmental attitude.

Harjeet Kaur (2012) found more favourable attitude towards environment after studying the subject of environmental education.

Kandir, Adalet, Yurt and Kalburan (2012) found that teacher educators got higher scores than pre-school teachers in terms of environmental attitude.

Environmental Attitude and Gender

Andrews and David Michael (1978) found no significant difference in the environmental attitude of men and women.

Hart and Nolan (1992) noticed that boys possessed better attitude towards environment compared to girls.

Sabhlok (1995) found that male and female teachers differed significantly on their environmental attitude and it was in favour of female teachers.

Abraham and Nair (1998) observed that the boys possessed better attitude towards environment compared to girls.

Jinarajan (1999) found that gender and socio-economic status of student teachers had an impact on environmental attitude.

Shabina (1999) reported a significant difference between male and female teachers in their environmental attitude; female teachers had better attitude.

Shaila (2003) found no gender difference with regard to environmental attitude.

Mercy and Arjunan (2005) revealed that boys had better environmental attitude than girls.

Shobeiri, *et.al.* (2006) observed a significant difference between environmental attitude of male and female student teachers.

Kumar and Patil (2007) observed no significant difference in the environmental attitude of male and female students.

Mustafa (2008) found that female elementary student teachers who had less than three brothers and sisters with high socio-economic status had more positive attitude than the other student teachers.

Larijani and Yeshodhara (2008) found that Indian women teachers had higher environmental attitude than men teachers towards environment.

Anna Uitto and Kalle Juuti (2011) found that girl's attitude was significantly more positive and their biocentric value was stronger than boys.

Mahbub Sarkar (2011) found that female students had favourable environmental attitude than boys.

Gulderen Saglam (2011) observed no gender difference in the environmental attitude of prospective teachers.

Environmental Attitude and Locality of Institutions

Hart and Nolan (1992) observed that rural and urban students differed significantly in their attitude towards environment, the difference being in favour of urban students.

Hampel, *et.al.* (1995) reported high environmental attitude in urban population compared to rural subjects.

Abraham and Nair (1998) reported high environmental attitude possessed by urban students.

Mercy and Arjunan (2005) stated that urban children had better environmental attitude than rural children.

Anna Uitto and Kalle Juuti (2011) observed no effect of locality on environmental attitude.

Mahbub Sarkar (2011) stated that rural girls had higher environmental attitude than their counterparts. Urban boys had greater environmental attitude than rural boys.

Environmental Attitude and Course Subjects

Bhattacharya (1977) found that the students of science had more environmental attitude than the students of non-science subjects.

Jinarajan (1999) found that the medium of instruction and subject had impact on environmental attitude.

Shaila (2003) found no significant difference among arts and science student teachers in their environmental attitude.

Sudeshana (2010) found that the mean scores of the student teachers belonging to science were nearly same with those belonging to humanities. The mean score of student teachers from Commerce was noticeably low, but not significantly different from any of the mean scores from Science and Humanities, as there was a significant effect of courses of study.

Anna Uitto and Kalle Juuti (2011) found that students interest in environmental issues, attitudes to environmental responsibility and biocentric values were enhanced through science education.

Environmental Attitude and Management of the Institution

Rou (1995) found that government school teachers had better environmental attitude than private school teachers.

Dinakara (2000) found no significant difference among the types of management on school teachers related to environmental attitude.

Shaila (2003) found no significant difference among types of school management on environmental attitude.

ENVIRONMENTAL ETHICS

The findings of the previous research related to environmental ethics are presented here under.

Environmental Ethics and Teachers

Aysun Oztuna (2009) found no significant difference in the levels of ecocentic approach statistically, in levels of apathy approach; significant differences were found between teacher education programmes; and it was also found that preservice teachers participated an environmental course had higher level of ecocentric concern.

Nuangchalerm (2009) found that environmental education teaching process using ethics infusion could develop environmental ethics among students at a high level and it can be supported by teachers through instructional strategies.

Samsun (2009) analysed certain non-anthropocentric approaches which differed according to class level and they were devoted to pre-service teachers developing positive view points about the environmental ethics and transferring these to their students.

Suresh Kotwani (2011) reported high environmental ethics among student teachers.

Wongchantra and Nuangchalerm (2011) found that environmental education teaching process using ethics infusion could develop student's environmental knowledge and environmental ethics at a higher level.

Suhane (2012) observed no significant difference in environmental ethics between in-service teachers and pre-service teachers.

Suhane (2012) observed a significant difference in environmental between pre-service teachers and teacher educators.

Marcela Espinosa-Pike and Edurne Aldazabal (2012) found that ethical training by teachers had a significant influence on their sensitivity towards the inclusion of ethics in graduate studies and the introduction of ethical aspects in their classes.

Environmental Ethics and Gender

Szagun and Mesenholl (1993) found that females scored higher than males in environmental ethics.

Raju (2007) found that higher secondary school male and female students had a significant difference between environmental ethics.

Nuangchalerm (2009) found that female students had higher score of environmental ethics than those of male students.

Suresh Kotwani (2011) found that female student teachers had more environmental ethics than male student teachers.

Wongchantra and Nuangchalerm (2011) found that female students had higher score of environmental knowledge and environmental ethics than those of male students.

Suhane (2012) observed a significant difference in environmental ethics between male in-service teachers and female in-service teachers.

Anjuli Suhane (2012) observed a significant difference in environmental ethics between male teacher educators and female teacher educators.

Marcela Espinosa-Pike and Edurne Aldazabal (2012) found that gender was not significant variable in terms of sensitivity towards the inclusion of ethics in graduate studies.

Environmental Ethics and Locality of the Institution

Raju (2007) found that rural higher secondary students had more environmental ethics than urban higher secondary students.

Suresh Kotwani (2011) observed no significant difference in rural and urban prospective teachers in their environmental ethics.

Environmental Ethics and Management of the Institution

Suresh Kotwani (2011) observed high level of environmental ethics among students studying in aided than un-aided institutes.

Environmental Ethics and Course Subject

Suhane (2012) observed no significant difference in environmental ethics between science and arts in-service teachers.

ASSOCIATION AMONG ENVIRONMENTAL AWARENESS, ENVIRONMENTAL ATTITUDE AND ENVIRONMENTAL ETHICS

David Michael (1978) found a positive relationship between the outdoor environmental education activities and environmental attitude.

Dhavan, Rawat and Veena (1997) found a moderate correlation between environmental attitude and environmental awareness after training. The environmental awareness and attitude of student teachers before training showed very low positive correlation.

Kumar, Mangal and Patil (2007) suggested that environmental education background helped to have better environmental attitude and ethics.

Heldref (2007) observed a positive relationship between the environmental knowledge and environmental attitudes of students.

Abdul Wahab (2008) observed a positive relationship between pro-environmental behaviour and pro-environmental attitude.

Sudeshana Lahiri (2010) observed a low correlation between environmental attitude and responsible environmental behaviour of student teachers.

Sara Peer and Daphne Goldman (2010) observed a positive relationship between environmental knowledge and environmental attitude of student teachers and the level of their mother's education.

Anna Uitto and Kalle Juuti (2011) observed a significant correlation between environmental attitude and environmental interest, but the correlation between environmental interest and environmental value was negligible.

Harjeet Kaur (2012) found that environmental awareness and environmental attitude were correlated to each other. The students who had higher environmental awareness had more favourable attitude towards environment.

These studies indicate that a study is needed on environmental awareness, environmental attitude and environmental ethics on teacher education students, as all of these are not directly concerned to the topic chosen for the study.

Thus, the review of the related literature helped to develop a clear insight into the problem and in selecting the present study, namely, "A Study of Environmental Awareness, Environmental Attitude and Environmental Ethics of Teacher Education Students".

3

DESIGN OF THE STUDY

Research is an endless quest for knowledge and an unending search for truth. It brings to light new knowledge or corrects previous errors and misconceptions and adds in an orderly way to the existing body of knowledge. The knowledge obtained by research is scientific and objective and is a matter of rational understanding, common verification and experience.

"Research is considered to be the more formal, systematic and intensive process of carrying on the scientific method of analysis. It involves a more systematic structure of investigation usually resulting in some sort of formal record of procedure and a report of results in conclusion". (John W. Best)

"Research is an honest, exhaustive, intelligent searching for facts and their meanings or implications with reference to a given problem. It is the process of arriving at dependable solutions to problems through the planned and systematic collection, analysis and interpretation of data. The best search is that which is reliable, verifiable and exhaustive, so that it provides information in which we have confidence". (P.M. Cook)

Research in education is needed to improve educational practices and policies. Many of our educationists are constantly engaged in research to find out effective methods of Instruction and satisfactory techniques of improving student behaviour. Research in education is also undertaken to develop suitable learning materials, satisfactory techniques of evaluation, more comfortable physical facilities and more efficient systems of educational management and administration.

Traverse considered educational research as that activity which is directed towards development of a science of behaviour in educational situations. He was of the opinion that the aim of research is to provide knowledge which will permit the educator to achieve these goals by the most effective methods.

Rummel has observed that since no two research undertakings are exactly alike, it is impossible to set forth any right formulation of method or procedure. There is a wide variation in the condition and circumstances which determine the objectives and nature of research problems in different fields. The purposes of a study may vary from researcher to researcher in terms where it is to be conducted and the applications to be made of it. In addition, great differences in the capacities and characteristics among the individuals who do research work are a proved fact. Thus, all methods differ portrayal in terms of formulae or standardization.

Considering its special advantages, and depending on the nature of the present study, the survey method has been chosen to study the environmental awareness, environmental attitude and environmental ethics of teacher education students studying in Hyderabad and Secunderabad twin cities and surrounding rural locations.

The formidable problem that follows the task of defining the research problem is the preparation of the design of the research project, popularly known as the 'Research Design'. Decision regarding what, where, when, how much, by what, concerning an inquiry or a research study constitute a research design.

A research design is the arrangement of conditions for collection and analysis of data in a manner that aims to combine relevance to research purpose with economy in procedure (Clair Selltiz and others, 1962). In fact, the research design is the conceptual structure within which research is conducted. It constitutes the blue print for the collection, measurement and analysis of data.

A good design is often characterized by objectives like flexibility, appropriateness, efficient, economical and so on. Generally, the design which minimizes bias and maximizes the reliability of the data collected and analysed, is considered a good design. The design, which gives the smallest experimental error, is supposed to be the best design in many investigations. Similarly, a design which yields maximal information and provides an opportunity for considering many different aspects of a problem is considered the most appropriate and efficient design in respect of many research problems. Thus, the question of good design is related to the purpose of the research problem and also to the nature of the problem to be studied.

For the present study, the following aspects have been discussed which are concerned with the design of the study. Research procedure includes the operational definitions of different terms used, the hypotheses that are framed for testing and the rationale of the formulated hypotheses. Selection of the sample includes the sampling techniques used, the reasons for selection of a particular sampling technique and the selection of samples according to variables. Selection of tools includes the selection of suitable tools for collection of data, description of the tools selected, testing their suitability for the present study, and the procedure followed in administering the tools to collect the data required for the study.

The normative survey method of investigation is very common in educational research, which attempts to describe and interpret what exists at present in the form of conditions, practices, processes, trends, effects, attitudes, beliefs, etc.

In normative survey method, the term 'normative' implies to the determination of normal or typical conditions or practices at present time and the term 'survey' indicates the gathering of data regarding current conditions. The normative survey method is an organized attempt to analyse, interpret and report the present status of a social institution, group or area. Survey studies collect information on what exists, on what we want, and on how to get there.

In the present study, normative survey method has been used. The normative survey of research is usually designed to obtain permanent and precise information concerning the current status of phenomena and whenever possible, to draw valid general conclusions from the facts discovered. It doesn't restrict itself only to fact finding but may often lead to research that results in the formulation of important principles of knowledge and solutions of significant problems concerning local, national and international issues.

OPERATIONAL DEFINITIONS OF KEY TERMS

The operational definitions of the important terms used in the present study are discussed for clarity of concepts.

Environment

Environment is the sum total of all conditions and influences that affect the development and life of an organism. Ecologists divide the environment into three parts – physical surroundings/abiotic environment, living organisms/biotic environment and meteorological factors/climatic factors.

Environmental Awareness

It is the sensitivity to the total environment and its allied problems. The development of environmental awareness means to understand the environmental problems and to develop critical thinking and problem-solving skill in the people.

Environmental Attitude

It is a set of values and feelings of concern for the environment and the motivation of active participation in environmental improvement and protection.

Environmental Ethics

It refers to the responsibility to understand the environmental consequences of our consumption and need to recognise our individual and social responsibility to conserve natural resources and protect the earth for future generations.

Teacher Education Students

The students who are studying B.Ed. and M.Ed. courses are referred to as teacher education students.

Bachelor of Education (B.Ed.)

Bachelor of Education is an under-graduate course meant for the students who wish to become teachers in secondary schools.

Master of Education (M.Ed.)

Master of Education is a post-graduate course meant for the students who wish to become teacher educators and wish to pursue research courses in education.

Private Teacher Education Colleges

The teacher education colleges managed by private organizations are in private teacher education colleges. These include private aided colleges and private un-aided teacher education colleges.

Government Teacher Education Colleges

The teacher education colleges managed by government are government teacher education colleges. These include government IASEs (Institutes of Advanced Study in Education) and CTEs (Colleges of Teacher Education).

Urban Teacher Education Colleges

The teacher education colleges located in urban areas are urban teacher education colleges.

Rural Teacher Education Colleges

The teacher education colleges located in rural areas are rural teacher education colleges.

Arts Students

The students pursuing Bachelor of Arts (B.A.), Bachelor of Commerce (B.Com.), Master of Arts (M.A.), Master of Commerce (M.Com.) (all social science subjects) are arts teacher education students.

Science Students

The students pursuing Bachelor of Science (B.Sc.), Master of Science (M.Sc.) (all the subjects of Physical Science,

Biological Science and Applied Sciences) are science teacher education students.

Age

The chronological age of the students of teacher education is taken into consideration and categorized into two age groups, *viz.*

1. Below 25 years and
2. Above 25 years.

Experience

The teaching experience is considered as the experience of the teacher education students as some students join teacher education courses after teaching for some time; the students then are categorized into two groups, *viz.*

1. Student teachers with teaching experience and
2. Student teachers with no teaching experience.

VARIABLES OF THE STUDY

A variable, as the name implies, is something which varies. This is the simplest and broadest way of defining a variable. However, a behaviour scientist attempts to define a variable more precisely and specifically. From his point of view, variables may be defined as those attributes of objects, events, things and beings which can be measured. In other words, variables are the characters or conditions that are manipulated, controlled or observed by the experimenter. Intelligence, anxiety, aptitude, adjustment, satisfaction, income, education, authoritarianism, achievements, etc., are the examples of variables commonly employed in psychology, sociology and education.

Variables are necessary requisites for any worthwhile research for the purpose of comparison. For the present study, the following variables are considered.

Gender

Now-a-days, women education has gained much importance as many women are getting into teaching profession. Teaching profession is very much suitable to women. As the psychological conditions, exposure to the society, concern towards living and non-living objects in the environment and exposure to environmentally sensitive experiences of male and female teacher education students vary differently. There may be a significant difference in the possession of environmental concepts by both of these groups. So, a comparison between male and female teacher education students will reveal of any difference that exists in the possession of environmental awareness, environmental attitude and environmental ethics.

Locality of the Teacher Education College

The rural and urban teacher education colleges differ in a variety of aspects such as exposure to environment, environmental problems, over consumption, over population, urban congestion, co-curricular activities, eco-clubs organization, environmental programmes, prevention measures, etc. These will definitely influence the environmental aspects of teacher education students. So, a comparison between rural and urban teacher education students will reveal of any difference that exists in possession of environmental awareness, environmental attitude and environmental ethics.

Subject of the Teacher Education Students

Arts and science teacher education students differ in participation in several activities related to the saving of environment, prevention of pollution, being aware of environmental issues, the course material, previous knowledge, sensitivity towards the environment, etc. So, a comparison between arts and science teacher education students will reveal of any difference that exists in possession of environmental awareness, environmental attitude and environmental ethics.

Management of the Teacher Education Colleges

In government teacher education colleges, appointment of teacher educators, service conditions, payment of scales, retirement benefits, administration, supervision, environmental educational programmes launched by UGC and NCERT, departmental facilities, etc., are very clear; whereas, in private colleges, the above aspects depend on the attitude of the management. These aspects will have considerable influence on teacher education students. So, a comparison between government and private teacher education students will reveal of any significant difference that exists in possession of environmental awareness, environmental attitude and environmental ethics.

Teaching Experience of Teacher Education Students

Teaching experience enriches a teacher in several aspects. It even enhances the awareness, attitude, skills and values in different dimensions. The environmental issues, problems, practical experiments, field work concerned with teaching environmental concepts and their implementation will help in gaining knowledge of environment. So, a comparison between teacher education students with some teaching experience and teacher education students with no teaching experience will reveal of any significant difference that exists in the possession of environmental awareness, environmental attitude and environmental ethics.

Age of Teacher Education Students

Age influences an individual's behaviour, maturation, way of thinking, level of reasoning, understanding the problems and issues related to environment. So, a comparison between teacher education students aged below 25 years and above 25 years will reveal of any significant difference that exists in the possession of environmental awareness, environmental attitude and environmental ethics.

Educational Qualification of Teacher Education Students

Bachelor of Education (B.Ed.) and Master of Education (M.Ed.) student teachers will differ as they possess the concepts of environment either as an optional paper in M.Ed. and as an unit in B.Ed. as a part of curriculum. Besides this, B.Ed. student teachers are exposed to life skills project and co-curricular project conducting eco-clubs, celebrating environmental day and some eco-friendly activities in the institutions. So, a comparison between B.Ed. and M.Ed. teacher education students will reveal of any significant difference that exists in the possession of environmental awareness, environmental attitude and environmental ethics.

HYPOTHESES OF THE STUDY

Hypothesis is a guess, a supposition or a tentative inference as to the existence of some fact, condition or relationship relative to some phenomenon which serves to explain such facts as already known to exist in a given area of research and to guide the search for the new truth.

A hypothesis may be defined as a proposition or a set of propositions set forth as an explanation for the occurrence of some specified group or phenomenon either asserted merely as a provisional conjecture to guide some investigation or accepted as highly probable in the light of established facts.

The following hypotheses were formulated in the present study.

Hypothesis 1: The teacher education students are not possessing high environmental awareness.

Hypothesis 1A: There is no significant difference in the environmental awareness of male and female teacher education students.

Hypothesis 1B: There is no significant difference in the environmental awareness of rural and urban teacher education students.

Hypothesis 1C: There is no significant difference in the environmental awareness of science and arts teacher education students.

Hypothesis 1D: There is no significant difference in the environmental awareness of government and private college teacher education students.

Hypothesis 1E: There is no significant difference in the environmental awareness of teacher education students with teaching experience and without teaching experience.

Hypothesis 1F: There is no significant difference in the environmental awareness of teacher education students aged below 25 years and aged above 25 years.

Hypothesis 1G: There is no significant difference in the environmental awareness of B.Ed. and M.Ed. teacher education students.

Hypothesis 2: The teacher education students are not possessing high environmental attitude.

Hypothesis 2A: There is no significant difference in the environmental attitude of male and female teacher education students.

Hypothesis 2B: There is no significant difference in the environmental attitude of rural and urban teacher education students.

Hypothesis 2C: There is no significant difference in the environmental attitude of science and arts teacher education students.

Hypothesis 2D: There is no significant difference in the environmental attitude of government and private college teacher education students.

Hypothesis 2E: There is no significant difference in the environmental attitude of teacher education students with teaching experience and without teaching experience.

Hypothesis 2F: There is no significant difference in the environmental attitude of teacher education students aged below 25 years and aged above 25 years.

Hypothesis 2G: There is no significant difference in the environmental attitude of B.Ed. and M.Ed. teacher education students.

Hypothesis 3: The teacher education students are not possessing high environmental ethics.

Hypothesis 3A: There is no significant difference in the environmental ethics of male and female teacher education students.

Hypothesis 3B: There is no significant difference in the environmental ethics of rural and urban teacher education students.

Hypothesis 3C: There is no significant difference in the environmental ethics of science and arts teacher education students.

Hypothesis 3D: There is no significant difference in the environmental ethics of government and private college teacher education students.

Hypothesis 3E: There is no significant difference in the environmental ethics of teacher education students with teaching experience and without teaching experience.

Hypothesis 3F: There is no significant difference in the environmental ethics of teacher education students aged below 25 years and aged above 25 years.

Hypothesis 3G: There is no significant difference in the environmental ethics of B.Ed. and M.Ed. teacher education students.

Hypothesis 4: There is no significant association among environmental awareness, environmental attitude and environmental ethics of teacher education students.

Hypothesis 4A: There is no significant association among environmental awareness, environmental attitude and environmental ethics of male and female teacher education students.

Hypothesis 4B: There is no significant association among environmental awareness, environmental attitude and environmental ethics of rural and urban teacher education students.

Hypothesis 4C: There is no significant association among environmental awareness, environmental attitude and environmental ethics of science and arts teacher education students.

Hypothesis 4D: There is no significant association among environmental awareness, environmental attitude and environmental ethics of government and private college teacher education students.

Hypothesis 4E: There is no significant association among environmental awareness, environmental attitude and environmental ethics of teacher education students with teaching experience and without teaching experience.

Hypothesis 4F: There is no significant association among environmental awareness, environmental attitude and environmental ethics of teacher education students aged below 25 years and aged above 25 years.

Hypothesis 4G: There is no significant association among environmental awareness, environmental attitude and environmental ethics of B.Ed. and M.Ed. teacher education students.

SAMPLE OF THE STUDY

After finalizing the variables of the present study, considerations were given to whether the entire population is to be made the subjects for data collection or a particular group is to be selected as a representative of the whole population. The entire population here refers to teacher education students studying in Hyderabad and Secunderabad twin cities and their surrounding rural areas.

Of the two techniques, the second one, namely, the selection of a group as a representative of the whole population was found to be more convenient and suitable. This technique leads to a considerable saving of time, effort and finance. As the number of teacher education students selected was small, it was possible to obtaine accurate and reliable results. As this sampling technique was more advantageous, it was selected for the collection of data.

In any educational research, various methods are utilised for selection and drawing of samples. After a detailed study of all these methods and considering the variables selected for the research work, the 'stratified sampling method' was found to be most suitable.

In the stratified sampling method, the entire population will be divided into smaller homogeneous groups or strata and then a sample is selected within each group. Every sampling unit in the population is placed in one of the strata prior to the selection of the sample so that the sum of the strata is identical with the population.

Stratified sampling method has certain merits as a technique of sampling. Auckoff has rightly said, "stratified sampling enables the researcher to make a composition of properties of the strata as well as to estimate population characteristics".

In this stratified sampling method, the investigator will have greater control over the selection of the sample when compared with random sampling. In random sampling, although every group has a chance of being selected and included in the sample, there is every possibility and sometimes it does happen, that certain important groups are left unrepresented. But, in stratified sampling method, no important group is likely to be left out.

Stratified sampling method is the ideal one when comparison between different variables has to be made. For example, if comparison has to be made between B.Ed. and M.Ed. teacher education students or rural and urban teacher education students, it would be very difficult to select the required number of units through any other method of sampling. If any other method is used, the problem of bias and prejudice creeps in.

Replacement of units is also possible in the stratified sampling method. Normally, if a particular unit is not accessible for a study, it is difficult to replace it by another, but in this method it is possible. Stephen states that stratification automatically brings about a replacement of persons lost in the sample, by persons of the same stratum, thus partly correcting the bias that would result if there were no replacement of loses. As the entire population is divided into particular strata, it is easy and convenient to replace an inaccessible case by an accessible one.

In stratified sampling method, much depends on stratification process. The following precautions were taken while stratifying the population. The variables involved in the study were taken note of; care was taken to see that each stratum in the universe was large enough in size so that selection of items could be done on random basis; the strata formed were definite and clear cut; each stratum was free from influence of the other; and there was no overlapping.

Before actually selecting the sample, certain fundamental principles were considered to make the sample scientific and clear cut. (Bhaskara Rao, 1989)

Firstly, the 'universe' was clearly defined. In the technical phraseology of research, the whole population out of which the samples are selected is known as the 'universe'. For the present research work, the universe includes all the teacher education students in Hyderabad and Secunderabad twin cities and their surrounding rural areas of Andhra Pradesh. The study was limited to a particular geographical area, *viz.* Hyderabad and Secunderabad twin cities, and their surrounding rural areas to facilitate appropriate sample selection and to avoid wastage of time and money.

Secondly, decision was made about the units of the sample. A unit of sample may be a house, a family, a group of individuals or a single individual. A good unit should possess the following characteristics.

(a) *Clarity:* The unit should be clearly defined in unambiguous terms. This would make the study easy and efficient. For the present research work, a sampling unit is defined as a teacher education student studying in any teacher education institute of Hyderabad and Secunderabad twin cities and their surrounding rural areas.

(b) *Suitability:* A good unit should be well suited to the problem under study. Since the problem is the study of the environmental ethics of the teacher education students, the unit selected is well suited to the problem.

(c) *Accessibility:* The unit selected should be easily accessible to the researcher. If the units selected are difficult to reach and if the researcher fails to make use of them, the study would be vitiated. The selected sampling units, *i.e.*, teacher education students, are easily accessible since they could be approached in any teacher education college.

Thirdly, availability of sample and preparation of the source list are very much essential. This is an important factor that makes representative selection possible. A source list is the list which contains the names of units of the universe from which the sample may be selected. It may exist even before the beginning of the project or it may be prepared afresh by the investigator herself. Without a source list, study through sampling method is not possible. For the present research work, a source list consisting of the names of the teacher education colleges in the Hyderabad and Secunderabad twin cities and their surrounding rural areas is used. Care was taken to see that the source list was up-to-date and valid and that there was no repetition of names of the teacher education colleges. This source list was found to be relevant and suitable because it included teacher education colleges as the study deals with the environmental awareness, environmental attitude and environmental ethics of teacher education students.

Besides considering these principles, it is extremely important to think about the size of the sample to be selected. If the sample is either too small or too large, it will make the study difficult and the results untenable. According to Parten, "An optimum sample in survey is one which fulfils the requirements of effective representatives, reliability and flexibility. The sample should be small enough to avoid intolerable sampling error." The size of sample for the present research work was decided after considering the following factors. (Bhaskara Rao, 1989)

1. Since an intensive study was planned, a very large number of samples were not selected. In the case of an intensive study, employing a very large number of samples is not very useful as it involves huge consumption of resources. A smaller sample will be more convenient.
2. The size and selection of the samples are also influenced by the nature of the Universe. If the universe is homogeneous, even a small-sized sample may yield dependable and required results. If the universe is heterogeneous, small-sized samples may not be useful. In case of the present study, the heterogeneous universe

was split into smaller homogeneous strata and then the samples were selected from these strata. For example, the teacher education students of Hyderabad and Secunderabad twin cities and their surrounding rural areas were broadly grouped under B.Ed. and M.Ed. teacher education students. A sample was selected from each of these groups.

3. The researcher needs to determine the number of groups to be formed. In case the number of groups proposed is large, the size of the samples shall have to be large. So that every group would be of proper size and suit the requirements of the study; in case the number of groups proposed is small, even small-sized samples can fulfill the requirement. In the case of the present study, the universe was divided into male and female teacher education students, rural and urban teacher education students, science and arts teacher education students, B.Ed. and M.Ed. teacher education students, etc. Since the number of groups was moderate, a reasonable sample was selected from each of these groups.
4. Practical considerations and accuracy will also play a vital role in determining the size of the sample. Every study is guided by certain practical considerations such as time, resources, accessibility of the data, etc. Generally, it is believed that a large-sized sample is more representative and usually produces accurate results. This, of course, mainly depends upon the technique of sampling used. If the sampling technique is scientific, even small-sized samples can produce dependable and accurate results. While selecting the size of the sample for the present study, practical considerations like the availability of resources and time were taken into consideration. Care was taken to make the sample selection technique as scientific as possible.
5. The size of the sample is also governed by the size of the tools to be used. In case the tools are short and the

questions asked pertain to certain limited factors, a large sample can be selected. In case the tools are large and the questions complicated, the sample should be small in size so that, from administrative point of view, the researcher may not be put to unnecessary troubles. In the present study, as the tools selected belong to affective domain, a very large sample was not selected.

6. The sampling method also determines the size of the sample. When random sampling method is used, the samples have to be large. On the other hand, if samples are selected through stratified sampling method, the reliability can be achieved even with the help of small-sized samples.

Taking these factors that influence the size of the sample into consideration, it was decided that an ideal sample would consist of 600 teacher education students. This sample is small enough to avoid unnecessary troubles and large enough to avoid intolerable sampling errors.

After deciding about the sampling method, the universe selected was divided into different strata. The variables chosen for the study were considered in dividing the universe. The sampling design employed here involved not only the stratification of the universe but also the random sampling technique to select the samples from within the stratum.

The total sample of 600 teacher education students, when split into groups, consisted of male teacher education students 300; female teacher education students 300; rural teacher education students 300; urban teacher education students 300; arts teacher education students 300; science teacher education students 300; government college teacher education students 300; private college teacher education students 300; teacher education students with teaching experience 300; teacher education students with no teaching experience 300; teacher education students aged below 25 years 300; teacher education students aged above 25 years 300; B.Ed. teacher education students 400; M.Ed. teacher education students 200

Table 3.1
Showing the Sample Size in the Present Study

S.No.	Variable	Classification	Sample	Total
1.	Gender	Male	300	600
		Female	300	
2.	Locality	Rural	300	600
		Urban	300	
3.	Subject	Art	300	600
		Science	300	
4.	Management	Government	300	600
		Private	300	
5.	Experience	Teaching Experience	300	600
		No Teaching Experience	300	
6.	Age	Below 25 year	300	600
		Above 25 year	300	
7.	Degree	B.Ed.	400	600
		M.Ed.	200	

TOOLS OF THE STUDY

A research tool plays a major role in any worthwhile research as it is the sole factor in determining the sound data and in arriving at perfect conclusions about the problem on hand, which, ultimately, helps in providing suitable remedial measures to solve the problem concerned.

The selection and use of the tools can be done in two ways. The first one is to construct a tool independently by the investigator for her own study. Here, there are many problems in doing so. Preparation and standardization of a perfect tool itself is a major task and one can safely say that it is a doctoral study. On construction of their own tools, Anand and Padma (1987) felt that "A note of caution has to be struck when a researcher develops a tool for his study by merely pooling some items and does not subject it to the sophisticated techniques of tool construction. The result would be then, obviously, a poor quality research". With this, one can say that preparation and standardization of tools is a major task, and one should take care of aspects like selection of area and sample, pooling up of statements related to the area, consulting the experts and application of sophisticated statistical techniques. (Bhaskara Rao, 1997).

The other way of selection and use of tools is right selection of tools from already standardized ones available in the field of study. Here also, locating the tools and identifying their usefulness to the study on hand is a tedious job. Even then, this technique is very useful when a research work is studied in depth, when the research work involves a good number of variables and when there is scarcity of time and other resources. Some people believe that some of the instruments available do not measure up to their standards. In some instances, consideration should be given to the logistics of the situation. Lacking time and financial resources for the construction of a test, many researchers can not expect to produce a better instrument. In these cases, the most logical procedure that one can follow is to choose the best instrument available for this purpose. (Bhaskara Rao, 1997)

Measurement of Environmental Awareness

Considering the flaws and merits of the selection of tools in either way, the researcher is interested in using the standardized tool as the present study involves a thorough study of environmental awareness of the students of teacher education. Hence, the investigator selected the 'Environmental Awareness Ability Measure', which was standardized by Dr. Praveen Kumar Jha, to measure the extent and degree of awareness of teacher education students.

Measurement of Environmental Attitude

Considering the flaws and merits of the selection of tools in either way, the researcher is interested in using the standardized tool as the present study involves a thorough study of environmental attitude of the students of teacher education. Hence, the investigator selected the 'Environmental Attitude Scale', which was standardized by Dr. Haseen Taj, to measure the extent and degree of attitude among the teacher education students.

Measurement of Environmental Ethics

The present study involves a thorough study of Environmental Ethics of the students of teacher education. Hence, the investigator selected 'Environmental Ethics Scale', which was standardized by Dr. Haseen Taj, to measure the ethics of teacher education students.

DATA COLLECTION

The investigator personally visited the selected teacher education colleges and administered the tests after taking permission from the administration. Before administering the test, clear instructions were given to the teacher education students and doubts were clarified. Tests were administered in ideal conditions. Thus, the data was collected from the total sample, scoring was done and scores were assigned to each teacher education student.

4

ANALYSIS OF THE DATA

The next steps in the process of research, after the collection of data, are organization, analysis and interpretation of data and formulation of conclusions and generalizations to get a meaningful picture out of the raw information collected. The analysis and interpretation of data involve the objective material in possession of the researcher and her/his subjective reactions and the desire to derive the inherent meanings in their relation to the problem from the data.

The mass data collected through the use of various tools, need to be systematized and organized, *i.e.*, edited, classified and tabulated before it can serve the purpose. Here, editing implies the checking of gathered data for accuracy, different categories of classes or heads for use; and tabulating denotes the recording of the classified material in accurate mathematical terms.

The analysis of data means studying the tabulated material in order to determine inherent facts or meanings. It involves breaking down the existing complex factors into simpler parts and putting the parts together in new arrangements for purpose of interpretation.

The present chapter, analysis of data, hence includes a study of the different techniques adopted for analysis and interpretation of data and the results of the analysis of data.

After finalizing the tools and sample for the study, the data was collected from six hundred (600) teacher education students.

The researcher used the Environmental Awareness Ability Measure (EAAM), standardized by Praveen Jha, to study the environmental awareness of teacher education students.

The investigator has used the Taj Environmental Attitude Scale (TEAS), standardized by Haseen Taj, to study the environmental attitude of teacher education students.

The investigator has used Environmental Ethics Scale (EES), stadardized by Haseen Taj, to study the environmental ethics of teacher education students.

As the collection of data was finished, it was analysed keeping the objectives and hypotheses of the study in view. The analysis of data was carried out in the following manner.

The present study included four major aspects, *viz.*, environmental awareness, environmental attitude, environmental ethics and the association among the above three aspects. From the tools, the total scores of environmental awareness, environmental attitude and environmental ethics were taken as raw scores for each teacher education student. These three types of raw scores were used as basic sources of data for the study of the said fourth aspect of the study. This raw data was put to statistical treatment.

Each of the three different aspects, *viz. (i)* environmental awareness, *(ii)* environmental attitude and *(iii)* environmental ethics of the study, were taken first into consideration individually. Later these, three aspects were tested for their association. The hypotheses framed under all four aspects were statistically tested and accordingly were accepted or rejected. The variables that were considered were – male teacher education students *vs.* female teacher education students, rural teacher education students versus urban teacher education students, science teacher education students *vs.* arts teacher education students, government college teacher education students *vs.* private college teacher education students, teacher education students with teaching experience *vs.* without teaching experience, teacher education students aged below 25 years versus aged above 25 years and B.Ed. teacher education students *vs.* M.Ed. teacher education students.

ENVIRONMENTAL AWARENESS OF TEACHER EDUCATION STUDENTS

The total score of environmental awareness of each teacher education student was taken to find out the level of environmental awareness possessed by each sub-sample as well as total sample of the study. The maximum score that a teacher education student can get was 51 and the minimum was 1. In the present study, the highest score secured was 38 and the lowest was 14.

For the purpose of classification of the level of environmental awareness possessed by the teacher education student, the environmental awareness level was divided into three categories, namely: *(i)* low environmental awareness (0-15), *(ii)* average environmental awareness (16-36), and *(iii)* high environmental awareness (37-51), as per the norms of EAAM.

The mean scores were used to identify the level of environmental awareness of teacher education students and to compare the sub-sample variation. The values of standard deviation were used to measure the spread or dispersion of scores in the distribution (Garret, 1979). The critical ratios were calculated to test the significant difference in the means of the sub-samples of each variable. The null hypotheses formulated for this study were accordingly accepted or rejected.

The chi-square test of independence was applied for comparing the experimentally obtained results with those to be expected theoretically.

Hypothesis 1

"The teacher education students are not possessing high environmental awareness".

To test the validity of hypothesis 1, the mean of the environmental awareness score was calculated.

Table 4.1
Environmental Awareness of Teacher Education Students

Sample	Sample Size	Mean	Standard Deviation
Whole	600	52.41	16.21

As per the Table 4.1, all the teacher education students possess average environmental awareness. The scores of environmental awareness were widely dispersed among teacher education students.

The chi-square test of independence was applied to test the divergence of observed results from those expected on the hypothesis of equal probability of distribution of trait in the sample.

Table 4.2
Distribution of Environmental Awareness in Teacher Education Students

Sample Size	Low	Average	High	Chi-Square Value
600	fo 86 fe 96	432 408	82 96	4.49#

df = 2, p at 0.01 level 9.210 *# Not significant at 0.01 level*

fo = frequency of observed or experimentally determined facts

fe = frequency of expected on some hypothesis

It is clear, from Table 4.2, that the distribution of environmental awareness scores in the whole sample was normal, as the chi-square value was not significant.

The hypothesis that "The teacher education students are not possessing high environmental awareness" can be rejected as the teacher education students were possessing average environmental awareness.

Hypothesis 1A

"There is no significant difference in the environmental awareness of male and female teacher education students".

To test the validity of the hypothesis 1A, the following calculations were made.

Table 4.3
Comparison of Environmental Awareness of Male and Female Teacher Education Students

Variable	Sample Size	Mean	Standard Deviation	Mean Difference	S.E.D.	C.R.
Male	300	37.84	15.78	2.09	1.35	1.55#
Female	300	39.93	17.43			

Critical Value at 0.01 level is 2.58 *# Not significant at 0.01 level*

As per Table 4.3, it is evident that there was no significant difference in the environmental awareness of male and female teacher education students. The environmental awareness dispersed widely in male and female teacher education students with some difference.

Further, the chi-square test was applied to test the divergence of observed results of male teacher education students and female teacher education students from those expected on the hypothesis of equal probability.

Table 4.4
Distribution of Environmental Awareness in Male and Female Teacher Education Students

Variable	Sample Size	Low	Average	High	Chi-Square Value
Male	300	fo 52	228	20	19.4*
		fe 48	204	48	
Female	300	fo 42	226	32	13.6*
		fe 48	204	48	

df = 2, p at 0.01 level 9.210 **Significant at 0.01 level*

As seen from Table 4.4, it can be concluded that the environmental awareness of male and female teacher education students was not normally distributed as the chi-square values were significant.

The hypothesis that "There is no significant difference in the environmental awareness of male and female teacher education students" can be accepted as both the sub-samples were possessing average environmental awareness with no significant difference.

Hypothesis 1B

"There is no significant difference in the environmental awareness of rural and urban teacher education students".

To test the validity of the hypothesis 1B, the following calculations were made.

Table 4.5

Comparison of Environmental Awareness of Rural and Urban Teacher Education Students

Variable	Sample Size	Mean	Standard Deviation	Mean Difference	S.E.D.	C.R.
Rural area	300	37.15	16.16	6.29	1.44	4.36*
Urban area	300	43.44	19.02			

Critical Value at 0.01 level is 2.58 ** Significant at 0.01 level*

As per Table 4.5, it is evident that there was a significant difference in the environmental awareness of rural and urban teacher education students, though both of them possess an average level of environmental awareness. Urban teacher education students had high environmental awareness than rural teacher education students. The environmental awareness dispersed widely in rural and urban teacher education students with some difference.

Further, the chi-square test was applied to test the divergence of observed results of rural and urban teacher education students from those expected on the hypothesis of equal probability.

As seen from Table 4.5, it can be concluded that the distribution of environmental awareness of rural teacher education students was not normally distributed as the chi-square value was significant. The distribution of environmental awareness of urban teacher education students was normal as the chi-square value was not significant.

Table 4.6
Distribution of Environmental Awareness in Rural and Urban Teacher Education Students

Variable	Sample Size	Low	Average	High	Chi-Square Value
Rural	300	fo 32 fe 48	228 204	40 48	9.47*
Urban	300	fo 30 fe 48	226 204	44 48	5.70#

df = 2, p at 0.01 level 9.210 ** Significant at 0.01 level*
 # Not significant at 0.01 level

The hypothesis that "There is no significant difference in the environmental awareness of rural and urban teacher education students" can be rejected as both the sub-samples were possessing average environmental awareness with a significant difference.

Hypothesis 1C

"There is no significant difference in the environmental awareness of science and arts teacher education students".

To test the validity of the hypothesis 1C, the following calculations were made.

Table 4.7
Comparison of Environmental Awareness of Science and Arts Teacher Education Students

Variable	Sample Size	Mean	Standard Deviation	Mean Difference	S.E.D.	C.R.
Science	300	44.31	18.26	8.58	1.36	6.30*
Arts	300	35.73	15.15			

Critical Value at 0.01 level is 2.58 ** Significant at 0.01 level*

As per Table 4.7, it is evident that there was a significant difference in the environmental awareness of science and arts teacher education students, though both of them possess average environmental awareness. Science teacher education students had high environmental awareness than arts teacher education students. The environmental awareness dispersed widely in science and arts teacher education students with some difference.

Further, the chi-square test was applied to test the divergence of observed results of science and arts teacher education students from those expected on the hypothesis of equal probability.

Table 4.8
Distribution of Environmental Awareness in Science and Arts Teacher Education Students

Variable	Sample Size	Low	Average	High	Chi-Square Value
Science	300	fo 32 fe 48	218 204	50 48	6.28#
Arts	300	fo 42 fe 48	230 204	28 48	12.39*

df = 2, p at 0.01 level 9.210

 # Not significant at 0.01 level
** Significant at 0.01 level*

As seen from Table 4.8, it can be concluded that the distribution of environmental awareness of science teacher education students was normal as the chi-square value was not significant. In arts teacher education students the distribution of environmental awareness was not normally distributed as the chi-square value was significant.

The hypothesis that "There is no significant difference in the environmental awareness of science and arts teacher education students" can be rejected as both the sub-samples were possessing average environmental awareness with a significant difference.

Hypothesis 1D

"There is no significant difference in the environmental awareness of government and private college teacher education students".

To test the validity of the hypothesis 1D, the following calculations were made.

Table 4.9
Comparison of Environmental Awareness of Government and Private College Teacher Education Students

Variable	Sample Size	Mean	Standard Deviation	Mean Difference	S.E.D.	C.R.
Government	300	38.73	15.41	2.36	1.214	1.94#
Private	300	36.37	14.37			

Critical Value at 0.01 level is 2.58 *# Not significant at 0.01 level*

As per Table 4.9, it is evident that there was a significant difference between government and private college teacher education students, as both of them were possessing average environmental awareness. The environmental awareness dispersed widely in government and private college teacher education students with some difference.

Further, the chi-square test was applied to test the divergence of observed results of government and private college teacher education students from those expected on the hypothesis of equal probability.

Table 4.10
Distribution of Environmental Awareness in Government and Private College Teacher Education Students

Variable	Sample Size	Low	Average	High	Chi-Square Value
Government	300	fo 29 fe 48	239 204	32 48	8.16*
Private	300	fo 40 fe 48	213 204	47 48	1.74

df = 2, p at 0.01 level is 9.210 *# Not significant at 0.01 level*

As seen from Table 4.10, it can be concluded that the distribution of environmental awareness of government college teacher education students and private college teacher education students was normal as the chi-square values were not significant.

The hypothesis that "There is no significant difference in the environmental awareness of government and private college teacher education students" can be accepted as both the sub-samples were possessing average environmental awareness with no significant difference.

Hypothesis 1E

"There is no significant difference in the environmental awareness of teacher education students with teaching experience and without teaching experience".

To test the validity of the hypothesis 1E, the following calculations were made.

Table 4.11
Comparison of Environmental Awareness of Teacher Education Students with Teaching Experience and without Teaching Experience

Variable	Sample Size	Mean	Standard Deviation	Mean Difference	S.E.D.	C.R.
Teaching experience	300	51.58	14.41	12.22	1.25	9.78*
No Teaching experience	300	39.36	16.26			

Critical Value at 0.01 level is 2.58 — ** Significant at 0.01 level*

As per Table 4.11, it is evident that there was a significant difference in the environmental awareness of teacher education students with teaching experience and without teaching experience, though both of them possess average environmental awareness. Teacher education students with teaching experience had high environmental awareness than their counter parts. The environmental awareness dispersed widely in both the sub-samples of teacher education students with some difference.

Further, the chi-square test was applied to test the divergence of observed results of teacher education students with teaching experience and without teaching experience from those expected on the hypothesis of equal probability.

As seen from Table 4.12, it can be concluded that the distribution of environmental awareness of teacher education students with teaching experience was not normally distributed as the chi-square value was significant.

Table 4.12

Distribution of Environmental Awareness of Teacher Education Students with Teaching Experience and without Teaching Experience

Variable	Sample Size	Low	Average	High	Chi-Square Value
Teaching experience	300	fo 23 fe 48	223 204	54 48	15.5*
No Teaching experience	300	fo 38 fe 48	217 204	45 48	3.0#

df = 2, p at 0.01 level is 9.210 ** Significant at 0.01 level*
 # Not significant at 0.01 level

The distribution of environmental awareness of teacher education students without teaching experience was normal as the chi-square values were not significant.

The hypothesis that "There is no significant difference in the environmental awareness of teacher education students with teaching experience and without teaching experience" can be rejected as both the sub-samples were possessing average environmental awareness with a significant difference.

Hypothesis 1F

"There is no significant difference in the environmental awareness of teacher education students aged below 25 years and above 25 years".

To test the validity of the hypothesis 1F, the following calculations were made.

Table 4.13

Comparison of Environmental Awareness of Teacher Education Students Aged Below 25 Years and Above 25 Years

Variable	Sample Size	Mean	Standard Deviation	Mean Difference	S.E.D.	C.R
Aged below 25 years	300	40.95	10.70	11.19	1.14	9.81*
Aged above 25 years	300	52.14	16.65			

Critical Value at 0.01 level is 2.58 ** Significant at 0.01 level*

As per Table 4.13, it is evident that there was a significant difference in the environmental awareness of teacher education students aged below 25 years and above 25 years, though both of them possess an average level of environmental awareness. Teacher education students aged above 25 years had high environmental awareness than aged below 25 years. The environmental awareness dispersed widely in the teacher education students aged below 25 years and above 25 years with some difference.

Further, the chi-square test was applied to test the divergence of observed results of teacher education students aged below 25 years and above 25 years from those expected on the hypothesis of equal probability.

Table 4.14
Distribution of Environmental Awareness of Teacher Education Students Aged Below 25 Years and Above 25 Years

Variable	Sample Size	Low	Average	High	Chi-Square Value
Aged below 25 years	300	fo 27 fe 48	251 204	22 48	33.9*
Aged above 25 years	300	fo 34 fe 48	224 204	42 48	6.7#

df = 2, p at 0.01 level is 9.210 ** Significant at 0.01 level*
 # Not significant at 0.01 level

As seen from Table 4.14, it can be concluded that the distribution of environmental awareness of teacher education students aged below 25 years was not normally distributed as the chi-square value was significant. The distribution of environmental awareness of teacher education students aged above 25 years was normal as the chi-square values were not significant.

The hypothesis that "There is no significant difference in the environmental awareness of teacher education students aged below 25 years and above 25 years" can be rejected as both the sub-samples were possessing average environmental awareness with a significant difference.

Hypothesis 1G

"There is no significant difference in the environmental awareness of B.Ed. and M.Ed. teacher education students".

To test the validity of the hypothesis 1G, the following calculations were made.

Table 4.15

Comparison of Environmental Awareness of B.Ed. and M.Ed. Teacher Education Students

Variable	Sample Size	Mean	Standard Deviation	Mean Difference	S.E.D.	C.R.
B.Ed.	400	49.70	17.41	11.42	1.33	8.5*
M.Ed	200	38.23	14.32			

Critical Value at 0.01 level is 2.58 ** Significant at 0.01 level*

As per Table 4.15, it is evident that there was a significant difference in the environmental awareness of B.Ed. and M.Ed. teacher education students, though both of them possess an average level of environmental awareness. B.Ed. teacher education students had high environmental awareness than M.Ed. teacher education students. The environmental awareness dispersed widely in B.Ed. and M.Ed. teacher education students with some difference.

Further, the chi-square test was applied to test the divergence of observed results of B.Ed. and M.Ed. teacher education students from those expected on the hypothesis of equal probability.

Table 4.16

Distribution of Environmental Awareness in B.Ed. and M.Ed. Teacher Education Students

Variable	Sample Size	Low	Average	High	Chi-Square Value
B.Ed.	400	fo 50 fe 64	290 272	60 64	4.5#
M.Ed	200	fo 18 fe 32	142 136	40 32	8.38#

df = 2, p at 0.01 level is 9.210 *# Not significant at 0.01 level*

As seen from Table 4.16, it can be concluded that the distribution of environmental awareness of B.Ed. and M.Ed. teacher education students was normal as the chi-square values were not significant.

The hypothesis that "There is no significant difference in the environmental awareness of B.Ed. and M.Ed. teacher education students" can be rejected as both the sub-samples were possessing average environmental awareness with a significant difference.

ENVIRONMENTAL ATTITUDE OF TEACHER EDUCATION STUDENTS

The total score of environmental attitude of each teacher education student was taken to find out the level of environmental attitude possessed by each sub-sample as well as total sample of the study. The maximum score that a teacher education student can get was 244 and the minimum was 61. In the present study, the highest score secured was 174 and the lowest was 100.

For the purpose of classification of the level of environmental attitude possessed by the teacher education student, the environmental attitude was assigned a weightage ranging from 4 (strongly agree) to 1 (strongly disagree) for favourable items. In case of unfavourable items, the scoring was reversed, *i.e.*, from 1 (strongly disagree) to 4 (strongly agree). The range of scores was from 61 to 244 divided into three categories, namely: *(i)* low environmental attitude (61-116), *(ii)* average environmental attitude (117-169), *(iii)* high environmental attitude (170-244), as per the norms of the scale.

The mean scores were used to identify the level of environmental attitude of teacher education students and to compare the sub-sample variation. The values of standard deviation were used to measure the spread or dispersion of scores in the distribution. The critical ratios were calculated to test the significant difference in the means of the sub-samples of each variable. The null hypotheses formulated for this study were accordingly accepted or rejected.

The chi-square test of independence was applied for comparing the experimentally obtained results with those to be expected theoretically.

Hypothesis 2

"The teacher education students are not possessing high environmental attitude".

To test the validity of hypothesis 2, the mean of environmental attitude score was calculated.

Table 4.17
Environmental Attitude of Teacher Education Students

Sample	Sample Size	Mean	Standard Deviation
Whole	600	161.82	16.23

As per the Table 4.17, all the teacher education students possess high environmental attitude. The scores of environmental attitude were widely dispersed among teacher education students.

The chi-square test of independence was applied to test the divergence of observed results from those expected on the hypothesis of equal probability of distribution of trait in the sample.

Table 4.18
Distribution of Environmental Attitude in Teacher Education Students

Sample Size	Low	Average	High	Chi-Square Value
600	fo 74 fe 96	427 408	99 96	6.01#

df = 2, p at 0.01 level 9.210 *# Not significant at 0.01 level*

It is clear, from Table 4.18, that the distribution of environmental attitude scores in the whole sample was normal, as the chi-square value was not significant

The hypothesis that "The teacher education students are not possessing high environmental attitude" can be rejected as the teacher education students were possessing high environmental attitude.

Hypothesis 2A

"There is no significant difference in the environmental attitude of male and female teacher education students".

To test the validity of the hypothesis 2A, the following calculations were made.

Table 4.19

Comparison of Environmental attitude of Male and Female Teacher Education Students

Variable	Sample Size	Mean	Standard Deviation	Mean Difference	S.E.D.	C.R.
Male	300	174.36	17.2	4.59	1.35	3.34*
Famale	300	178.95	16.5			

Critical Value at 0.01 level is 2.58 ** Significant at 0.01 level*

As per Table 4.19, it is evident that there was a significant difference in the environmental attitude of male and female teacher education students, though both of them possess high environmental attitude. Female teacher education students had high environmental attitude than male teacher education students. The environmental attitude dispersed widely in male and female teacher education students with some difference.

Further, the chi-square test was applied to test the divergence of observed results of male teacher education students and female teacher education students from those expected on the hypothesis of equal probability.

Table 4.20

Distribution of Environmental Attitude in Male and Female Teacher Education Students

Variable	Sample Size	Low	Average	High	Chi-Square Value
Male	300	fo 54 fe 48	190 204	56 48	3.04#
Female	300	fo 34 fe 48	222 204	44 48	5.83#

df = 2, p at 0.01 level 9.210 *# Not significant at 0.01 level*

As per Table 4.20, it is evident that the environmental attitude of male and female teacher education students was normally distributed as the chi-square values were not significant.

The hypothesis that "There is no significant difference in the environmental attitude of male and female teacher education students" can be rejected as both the sub-samples were possessing high environmental attitude with a significant difference.

Hypothesis 2B

"There is no significant difference in the environmental attitude of rural and urban teacher education students".

To test the validity of the hypothesis 2B, the following calculations were made.

Table 4.21
Comparison of Environmental Attitude of Rural and Urban Teacher Education Students

Variable	Sample Size	Mean	Standard Deviation	Mean Difference	S.E.D.	C.R.
Rural	300	172.79	15.2	6.63	1.20	5.52*
Urban	300	179.42	14.3			

Critical Value at 0.01 level is 2.58 ** Significant at 0.01 level*

As per Table 4.21, it is evident that there was a significant difference in the environmental attitude of rural and urban teacher education students, though both of them possess high environmental attitude. Urban teacher education students had high environmental attitude than rural teacher education students. The environmental attitude dispersed widely in rural and urban teacher education students with some difference.

Further, the chi-square test was applied to test the divergence of observed results of rural and urban teacher education students from those expected on the hypothesis of equal probability.

Table 4.22
Distribution of Environmental attitude in Rural and Urban Teacher Education Students

Variable	Sample Size	Low	Average	High	Chi-Square Value
Rural	300	fo 56	170	74	20.95*
		fe 48	204	48	
Urban	300	fo 22	211	67	21.74*
		fe 48	204	48	

df = 2, p at 0.01 level 9.210 ** Significant at 0.01 level*

As per Table 4.22, the distribution of environmental attitude in rural and urban teacher education students was not normal as the chi-square values were significant.

The hypothesis that "There is no significant difference in the environmental attitude of rural and urban teacher education students" can be rejected as both the sub-samples were possessing high environmental attitude with a significant difference.

Hypothesis 2C

"There is no significant difference in the environmental attitude of science and arts teacher education students".

To test the validity of the hypothesis 2C, the following calculations were made.

Table 4.23
Comparison of Environmental Attitude of Science and Arts Teacher Education Students

Variable	Sample Size	Mean	Standard Deviation	Mean Difference	S.E.D.	C.R.
Science	300	180.80	16.2	21.12	1.38	15.30*
Art	300	159.65	17.7			

Critical Value at 0.01 level is 2.58 ** Significant at 0.01 level*

As per Table 4.23, it was evident that there was a significant difference in the environmental attitude of science and arts teacher education students, though both of them possess high environmental attitude. Science teacher education students had high environmental attitude than arts teacher education students. The environmental attitude dispersed widely in science and arts teacher education students with some difference.

Further, the chi-square test was applied to test the divergence of observed results of science and arts teacher education students from those expected on the hypothesis of equal probability.

Table 4.24
Distribution of Environmental Attitude in Science and Arts Teacher Education Students

Variable	Sample Size	Low	Average	High	Chi-Square Value
Science	300	fo 53	185	62	8.4#
		fe 48	204	48	
Art	300	fo 57	188	55	3.95#
		fe 48	204	48	

df = 2, p at 0.01 level 9.210 *# Not significant at 0.01 level*

As per Table 4.24, it can be concluded that the distribution of environmental attitude in science and arts teacher education students was normal as the chi-square values were not significant.

The hypothesis that "There is no significant difference in the environmental attitude of science and arts teacher education students" can be rejected as both the sub-samples were possessing high environmental attitude with a significant difference.

Hypothesis 2D

"There is no significant difference in the environmental attitude of government and private college teacher education students".

To test the validity of the hypothesis 2D, the following calculations were made.

Table 4.25
Comparison of Environmental Attitude of Government and Private College Teacher Education Students

Variable	Sample Size	Mean	Standard Deviation	Mean Difference	S.E.D.	C.R.
Government	300	165.5	17.5	2.3	1.44	1.59#
Private	300	167.2	17.9			

Critical Value at 0.01 level is 2.58 *# Not significant at 0.01 level*

As per Table 4.25, it is evident that there was no significant difference in the environmental attitude of government and private college teacher education students, as both of them possess high environmental attitude. The environmental attitude dispersed widely in government and private college teacher education students with some difference.

Further, the chi-square test was applied to test the divergence of observed results of government and private college teacher education students from those expected on the hypothesis of equal probability.

Table 4.26
Distribution of Environmental Attitude in Government and Private College Teacher Education Students

Variable	Sample Size	Low	Average	High	Chi-Square Value
Government	300	fo 52	188	60	4.58#
		fe 48	204	48	
Private	300	fo 60	166	74	24.1*
		fe 48	204	48	

df = 2, p at 0.01 level is 9.210 ** Significant at 0.01 level*
 # Not significant at 0.01 level

As seen from Table 4.26, it can be concluded that the distribution of environmental attitude of government college teacher education students was normal as the chi-square value was not significant. Distribution of environmental attitude of private college teacher education students was not normal as the chi-square values were significant.

The hypothesis that "There is no significant difference in the environmental attitude of government and private college teacher education students" can be accepted as both the sub-samples were possessing high environmental attitude without any significant difference.

Hypothesis 2E

"There is no significant difference in the environmental attitude of teacher education students with teaching experience and without teaching experience".

To test the validity of the hypothesis 2E, the following calculations were made.

Table 4.27

Comparison of Environmental Attitude of Teacher Education Students with Teaching Experience and without Teaching Experience

Variable	Sample Size	Mean	Standard Deviation	Mean Difference	S.E.D.	C.R.
Teaching experience	300	177.5	18.6	9	1.46	6.16*
No Teaching experience	300	168.5	17.3			

Critical Value at 0.01 level is 2.58   ** Significant at 0.01 level*

As per Table 4.27, it is evident that there was a significant difference in the environmental attitude of teacher education students with teaching experience and without teaching experience, though both of them possess high environmental attitude. Teacher education students with teaching experience had high environmental attitude than the teacher education students without teaching experience. The environmental attitude dispersed widely in teaching education students with teaching experience and without teaching experience with some difference.

Further, the chi-square test was applied to test the divergence of observed results of teacher education students with teaching experience and without teaching experience from those expected on the hypothesis of equal probability.

Table 4.28
Distribution of Environmental Attitude in Teacher Education Students with Teaching Experience and without Teaching Experience

Variable	Sample Size	Low	Average	High	Chi-Square Value
Teaching experience	300	fo 54 fe 48	187 204	59 48	4.68#
No Teaching experience	300	fo 50 fe 48	209 204	41 48	3.48#

df = 2, p at 0.01 level is 9.210 *# Not significant at 0.05 level*

As seen from Table 4.28, it can be concluded that the distribution of environmental attitude of teacher education students with teaching experience and without teaching experience was normal as the chi-square values were not significant.

The hypothesis that "There is no significant difference in the environmental attitude of teacher education students with teaching experience and without teaching experience" can be rejected as both the sub-samples were possessing high environmental attitude with a significant difference.

Hypothesis 2F

"There is no significant difference in the environmental attitude of teacher education students aged below 25 years and above 25 years".

To test the validity of the hypothesis 2F, the following calculations were made.

As per Table 4.29, it is evident that there was no significant difference in the environmental attitude of teacher education students aged below 25 years and above 25 years, though both of them possess high environmental attitude. The environmental attitude dispersed widely in teacher education students aged below 25 years and above 25 years with some difference.

Table 4.29
Comparison of Environmental Attitude of Teacher Education Students Aged Below 25 Years and Above 25 Years

Variable	Sample Size	Mean	Standard Deviation	Mean Difference	S.E.D.	C.R.
Aged below 25 years	300	149.01	18.1	2.49	1.48	1.68#
Aged above 25 years	300	150.5	18.3			

Critical Value at 0.01 level is 2.58 *# Not significant at 0.01 level*

Further, the chi-square test was applied to test the divergence of observed results of teacher education students aged below 25 years and above 25 years from those expected on the hypothesis of equal probability.

Table 4.30
Distribution of Environmental Attitude in Teacher Education Students Aged Below 25 Years and Above 25 Years

Variable	Sample Size	Low	Average	High	Chi-Square Value
Aged below 25 years	300	fo 44 fe 48	216 204	40 48	2.36#
Aged above 25 years	300	fo 50 fe 48	194 204	56 48	1.90#

df = 2, p at 0.01 level is 9.210 *# Not significant at 0.01 level*

As seen from Table 4.30, it can be concluded that the distribution of environmental attitude of teacher education students aged below 25 years and above 25 years was normal as the chi-square values were not significant.

The hypothesis that "There is no significant difference in the environmental attitude of teacher education students aged below 25 years and above 25 years" can be accepted as both the sub-samples were possessing high environmental attitude without any significant difference.

Hypothesis 2G

"There is no significant difference in the environmental attitude of B.Ed. and M.Ed. teacher education students".

To test the validity of the hypothesis 2G, the following calculations were made.

Table 4.31
Comparison of Environmental Attitude of B.Ed. and M.Ed. Teacher Education Students

Variable	Sample Size	Mean	Standard Deviation	Mean Difference	S.E.D.	C.R.
B.Ed.	400	164.7	18.1	5.5	1.46	3.64*
M.Ed	200	170.2	17.2			

Critical Value at 0.01 level is 2.58   ** Significant at 0.01 level*

As per Table 4.31, it is evident that there was a significant difference in the environmental attitude of B.Ed. and M.Ed. teacher education students, though both of them possess high environmental attitude. M.Ed. teacher education students had high environmental attitude than B.Ed. teacher education students. The environmental attitude dispersed widely in B.Ed. and M.Ed. teacher education students with some difference.

Further, the chi-square test was applied to test the divergence of observed results of B.Ed. and M.Ed. teacher education students from those expected on the hypothesis of equal probability.

Table 4.32
Distribution of Environmental Attitude in B.Ed. and M.Ed. Teacher Education Students

Variable	Sample Size	Low	Average	High	Chi-Square Value
B.Ed.	400	fo 60 fe 64	280 272	60 64	2.73#
M.Ed.	200	fo 20 fe 32	148 136	42 32	8.67#

df = 2, p at 0.01 level is 9.210   *# Not significant at 0.01 level*

As seen from Table 4.32, it can be concluded that the distribution of environmental attitude of B.Ed. and M.Ed. teacher education students was normal as the chi-square values were not significant.

The hypothesis that "There is no significant difference in the environmental attitude of B.Ed. and M.Ed. teacher education students" can be rejected as both the sub-samples were possessing average environmental attitude with a significant difference.

ENVIRONMENTAL ETHICS OF TEACHER EDUCATION STUDENTS

The total score of environmental ethics of each teacher education student was taken to find out the level of environmental ethics possessed by each sub-sample as well as total sample of the study. The maximum score that a teacher education student can score was 135 and the minimum was 35. In the present study, the highest score secured was 110 and the lowest was 35.

For the purpose of classification of the level of environmental ethics possessed by the teacher education student, the environmental ethics range of scores from 34 to 135 was divided into four categories namely: *(i)* below average environmental ethics (35-50), *(ii)* average environmental ethics (51-74), *(iii)* above average environmental ethics (75-90), *(iv)* High environmental ethics (91-135) as per the norms of EES.

The mean scores were used to identify the level of environmental ethics of teacher education students and to compare the sub-sample variation. The values of standard deviation were used to measure the spread or dispersion of scores in the distribution. The critical ratio was calculated to test the significant difference in the means of the sub-samples of each variable. The null hypotheses formulated for this study were accordingly accepted or rejected.

The chi-square test of independence was applied for comparing the experimentally obtained results with those to be expected theoretically.

Hypothesis 3

"The teacher education students are not possessing high environmental ethics".

To test the validity of hypothesis 3, the mean of the environmental ethics score was calculated.

Table 4.33
Environmental Ethics of Teacher Education Students

Sample	Sample Size	Mean	Standard Deviation
Whole	600	63.21	14.45

As per Table 4.33, all the teacher education students possess average environmental ethics. The scores of environmental ethics were widely dispersed among teacher education students.

The chi-square test of independence was applied to test the divergence of observed results from those expected on the hypothesis of equal probability of distribution of trait in the sample.

Table 4.34
Distribution of Environmental Ethics in Teacher Education Students

Sample Size	Low	Average	High	Chi-Square Value
600	fo 110 fe 96	430 408	60 96	*16.72

df = 2, p at 0.01 level 9.210 ** Significant at 0.01 level*

It is clear, from Table 4.34, that the distribution of environmental ethics scores in the whole sample was not normal.

The hypothesis that "The teacher education students are not possessing high environmental ethics" can be accepted as the teacher education students were possessing average environmental ethics.

Hypothesis 3A

"There is no significant difference in the environmental ethics of male and female teacher education students".

To test the validity of the hypothesis 3A, the following calculations were made.

Table 4.35

Comparison of Environmental Ethics of Male and Female Teacher Education Students

Variable	Sample Size	Mean	Standard Deviation	Mean Difference	S.E.D.	C.R.
Male	300	66.21	13.6	1.39	1.14	#1.21
Female	300	67.6	14.6			

Critical value at 0.01 level is 2.58 *# Not significant at 0.01 level*

It is clear, from Table 4.35, that there was no significant difference in the environmental ethics of male and female teacher education students, though both of them possess average environmental ethics. The environmental ethics dispersed widely in male and female teacher education students with some difference.

Further, the chi-square test was applied to test the divergence of observed results of male and female teacher education students from those expected on the hypothesis of equal probability.

Table 4.36

Distribution of Environmental Ethics in Male and Female Teacher Education Students

Variable	Sample Size	Low	Average	High	Chi-Square Value
Male	300	fo 62 fe 48	200 204	38 48	#6.23
Female	300	fo 51 fo 48	209 204	40 48	#1.63

df – 2 p at 0.01 level is 9.210 *# Not Significant at 0.05 level*

As per Table 4.36, it is evident that the distribution of environmental ethics of male and female teacher education students was normal as the Chi-square value was not significant.

The hypothesis that "There is no significant difference in the environmental ethics of male and female teacher education students" can be accepted as both the sub-samples were possessing average environmental ethics without any significant difference.

Hypothesis 3B

"There is no significant difference in the environmental ethics of rural and urban teacher education students."

To test the validity of the hypothesis 3B, the following calculations were made.

Table 4.37
Comparison of Environmental Ethics of Rural and Urban Teacher Education Students

Variable	Sample Size	Mean	Standard Deviation	Mean Difference	S.E.D.	C.R.
Male	300	63.58	15.2	6.63	1.196	*5.54
Female	300	70.21	14.1			

Critical value at 0.01 level is 2.58 ** Significant at 0.01 level*

As per Table 4.37, it is evident that there was a significant difference in the environmental ethics of rural and urban teacher education students, though both of them possess average environmental ethics. Urban teacher education students had high environmental ethics than rural teacher education students. The environmental ethics dispersed widely in rural and urban teacher education students with some difference.

Further, the chi-square test was applied to test the divergence of observed results of rural and urban teacher education students from those expected on the hypothesis of equal probability.

Table 4.38
Distribution of Environmental Ethics in Rural and Urban Teacher Education Students

Variable	Sample Size	Low	Average	High	Chi-Square Value
Rural	300	fo 40 fe 48	229 204	31 48	*10.41
Urban	300	fo 30 fe 48	230 204	40 48	*11.39

df = 2, p at 0.01 level is 9.210 ** Significant at 0.01 level*

Table 4.38 revealed that the distribution of environmental ethics of rural and urban teacher education students was not normal as the Chi-square values were significant.

The hypothesis "There is no significant difference in the environmental ethics of rural and urban teacher education students" can be rejected as both the samples were possessing average environmental ethics with a significant difference between them.

Hypothesis 3C

"There is no significant difference in the environmental ethics of science and arts teacher education students".

To test the validity of the hypothesis 3C, the following calculations were made.

Table 4.39

Comparison of Environmental Ethics of Science and Arts Teacher Education Students

Variable	Sample Size	Mean	Standard Deviation	Mean Difference	S.E.D.	C.R.
Science	300	68.00	13.1	3.1	1.18	*2.62
Art	300	64.90	15.8			

Critical value at 0.01 level is 2.58   ** Significant at 0.01 level*

As per Table 4.39, it is evident that there was a significant difference in the environmental ethics of science and arts teacher education students, though both of them possess average environmental ethics. Science teacher education students had high environmental ethics than arts teacher education students. The environmental ethics dispersed widely in science and arts teacher education students with some difference.

Further, the Chi-square test was applied to test the divergence of observed results of science and arts teacher education students from those expected on the hypothesis of equal probability.

As per Table 4.40, it can be concluded that the distribution of science and arts teacher education students was not normal as the chi-square value was significant.

Table 4.40
Distribution of Environmental Ethics in Science and Arts Teacher Education Students

Variable	Sample Size	Low	Average	High	Chi-Square Value
Science	300	fo 20 fe 48	222 204	58 48	*19.8
Arts	300	fo 40 fe 48	228 204	30 48	*9.46

df=2, p at 0.01 level is 9.210 ** Significant at 0.01*

The hypothesis that "There is no significant difference in the environmental ethics of science and arts teacher education students" can be rejected as both the sub-samples were possessing average environmental ethics with a significant difference.

Hypothesis 3D

"There is no significant difference in the environmental ethics of government and private college teacher education students".

To test the validity of hypothesis 3D, the following calculations were made.

Table 4.41
Comparison of Environmental Ethics of Government and Private College Teacher Education Students

Variable	Sample Size	Mean	Standard Deviation	Mean Difference	S.E.D.	C.R.
Government	300	65.72	14.3	1.28	1.19	#1.07
Private	300	67.00	14.9			

Critical Value at 0.01 level is 2.58 *# Not significant at 0.01 level*

As per Table 4.41, it is evident that there was no significant difference in the environmental ethics of government and private college teacher education students as both of them possess average environmental ethics. The environmental ethics dispersed widely in government and private college teacher education students with some difference.

Further, the chi-square test was applied to test the divergence of observed results of government and private teacher education students from those expected on the hypothesis of equal probability.

Table 4.42

Distribution of Environmental Ethics in Government and Private College Teacher Education Students

Variable	Sample Size	Low	Average	High	Chi-Square Value
Government	300	fo 46 fe 48	215 204	39 48	#2.35
Private	300	fo 44 fe 48	221 204	35 48	#5.25

df = 2, p at 0.01 level is 9.210 *# Not significant at 0.01 level*

As seen from the Table 4.42, it can be concluded that the distribution of environmental ethics of government and private college teacher education students was normal.

The hypothesis that "There is no significant difference in the environmental ethics of government and private college teacher education students" can be accepted as both the sub-samples were possessing average environmental ethics without any significant difference.

Hypothesis 3E

"There is no significant difference in the environmental ethics of teacher education students with teaching experience and without teaching experience".

To test the validity of the hypothesis 3E, the following calculations were mode.

As per Table 4.43, it is evident that there was no significant difference in the environmental ethics of teacher education students with teaching experience and without teaching experience, though both of them possess average environmental ethics. The environmental ethics dispersed widely in teacher education students with and without teaching experience with some difference.

Table 4.43
Comparison of Environmental Ethics of Teacher Education Students with Teaching Experience and without Teaching Experience

Variable	Sample Size	Mean	Standard Deviation	Mean Difference	S.E.D.	C.R.
Teaching experience	300	72.42	13.4	2.7	1.20	2.25#
No Teaching experience	300	69.72	16.1			

Critical Value at 0.01 level is 2.58 *# Not significant at 0.01 level*

Further, the Chi-square test was applied to test the divergence of observed results of teacher education students with teaching experience and without teaching experience from those expected on the hypothesis of equal probability.

Table 4.44
Distribution of Environmental Ethics of Teacher Education Students with Teaching Experience and without Teaching Experience

Variable	Sample Size	Low	Average	High	Chi-Square Value
Teaching experience	300	fo 42 fe 48	221 204	37 48	#4.68
No Teaching experience	300	fo 57 fe 48	201 204	42 48	#2.39

df = 2, p at 0.01 level is 9.210 *# Not significant at 0.01 level*

As seen from the Table 4.44, it can be concluded that the distribution of environmental ethics of teacher education students with teaching experience and without teaching experience was normal as the chi-square values were not significant.

The hypothesis that "There is no significant difference in the environmental ethics of teacher education students with teaching experience and without teaching experience" can be accepted as both the sub-samples were possessing average environmental ethics without any significant difference.

Hypothesis 3F

"There is no significant difference in the environmental ethics of teacher education students aged below 25 years and above 25 years".

To test the validity of the hypothesis 3F, the following calculations were made.

Table 4.45
Comparison of Environmental Ethics of Teacher Education Students Aged Below 25 Years and Above 25 Years

Variable	Sample Size	Mean	Standard Deviation	Mean Difference	S.E.D.	C.R.
Aged below 25 years	300	65.10	15.4	2.49	1.31	#1.90
Aged above 25 years	300	67.59	16.7			

Critical value at 0.01 level is 2.58 *# Not significant at 0.01 level*

As per Table 4.45, it is evident that there was no significant difference in the environmental ethics of teacher education students aged below 25 years and aged above 25 years, though both of them possess average environmental ethics. The environmental ethics dispersed widely in teacher education students aged below 25 years and above 25 years with some difference.

Further, the chi-square test was applied to test the divergence of observed results of teacher education students aged below 25 years and above 25 years from those expected on the hypothesis of equal probability.

As seen from Table 4.46, it can be concluded that the distribution of environmental ethics of teacher education students aged below 25 years was not normal as the chi-square value was significant whereas in teacher education students aged above 25 years, it was normally distributed as the chi-square value was not significant.

The hypothesis that "There is no significant difference in the environmental ethics of teacher education students

Table 4.46
Distribution of Environmental Ethics in Teacher Education Students Aged Below 25 Years and Above 25 Years

Variable	Sample Size	Low	Average	High	Chi-Square Value
Aged below 25 years	300	fo 30 fe 48	236 204	34 48	*15.8
Aged above 25 years	300	fo 60 fe 48	200 204	40 48	#4.40

df = 2. p at 0.01 level is 9.210 ** Significant at 0.01 level*
 # Not Significant at 0.01 level

aged below 25 years and above 25 years" can be accepted as both the sub-samples were possessing average environmental ethics without any significant difference.

Hypothesis 3G

"There is no significant difference in the environmental ethics of B.Ed. and M.Ed. teacher education students".

To test the validity of the hypothesis 3G, the following calculations were made.

Table 4.47
Comparison of Environmental Ethics of B.Ed. and M.Ed. Teacher Education Students

Variable	Sample Size	Mean	Standard Deviation	Mean Difference	S.E.D.	C.R.
B.Ed.	400	67.94	14.7	3.11	1.2	*2.59
M.Ed.	200	64.83	14.3			

Critical value at 0.01 level is 2.58 ** Significant at 0.01 level*

As per the Table 4.47, it is evident that there was a significant difference in the environmental ethics of B.Ed. and M.Ed. teacher education students, though both of them possess average environmental ethics. B.Ed. teacher education students had high environmental ethics than M.Ed. teacher education students. The environmental ethics dispersed widely in B.Ed. and M.Ed. teacher education students with some difference.

Further, the chi-square test was applied to test the divergence observed results of B.Ed. and M.Ed. teacher education students from those expected on the hypothesis of equal probability.

Table 4.48
Distribution of Environmental Ethics in B.Ed. and M.Ed. Teacher Education Students

Variable	Sample Size	Low	Average	High	Chi-Square Value
B.Ed.	400	fo 46 fe 64	320 272	34 64	*27.53
M.Ed.	200	fo 40 fe 32	135 136	25 32	#3.5

df = 2, p at 0.01 level is 9.210 — ** Significant at 0.01 level*; *# Not Significant at 0.01 level*

As seen from the Table 4.48, it can be concluded that the distribution of environmental ethics of B.Ed. teacher education students was not normal as the chi-square value was significant, whereas environmental ethics of M.Ed. teacher education students was normally distributed as the chi-square value was not significant.

The hypothesis that "There is no significant difference in the environmental ethics of B.Ed. and M.Ed. teacher education students" can be rejected as both the sub-samples were possessing average environmental ethics with a significant difference.

ASSOCIATION AMONG ENVIRONMENTAL AWARENESS, ENVIRONMENTAL ATTITUDE AND ENVIRONMENTAL ETHICS OF TEACHER EDUCATION STUDENTS

The chi-square test was applied to find out the association among environmental awareness, environmental attitude and environmental ethics of teacher education students.

Hypothesis 4

"There is no significant association among environmental awareness, environmental attitude and environmental ethics of teacher education students".

To test the validity of the hypothesis 4, the chi-square values were computed.

Table 4.49
Association among Environmental Awareness, Environmental Attitude and Environmental Ethics of Teacher Education Students

Sample Size	Environmental Awareness with Environmental Attitude	Environmental Attitude with Environmental Ethics	Environmental Ethics with Environmental Awareness
600	#4.909	*37.15	*13.30

df = 4, p at 0.01 level is 13.277   ** Significant at 0.01 level*
 # Not significant at 0.01 level

The chi-square values in Table 4.49 show that there was a significant association between environmental attitude and environmental ethics and environmental ethics and environmental awareness of teacher education students. There was no significant association between environmental awareness and environmental attitude of teacher education students and hence these two traits are independent of each other.

The hypothesis that "There is no significant association among environmental awareness, environmental attitude and environmental ethics of teacher education students" can be rejected as a significant association was found between environmental attitude and environmental ethics and environmental ethics and environmental awareness, though no significant association was found between environmental awareness and environmental attitude of teacher education students.

Hypothesis 4A

"There is no significant association among environmental awareness, environmental attitude and environmental ethics of male and female teacher education students".

To test the validity of hypothesis 4A, the chi-square values were computed.

Table 4.50
Association among Environmental Awareness, Environmental Attitude and Environmental Ethics of Male and Female Teacher Education Students

Variable	Sample Size	Environmental Awareness with Environmental Attitude	Environmental Attitude with Environmental Ethics	Environmental Ethics with Environmental Awareness
Male	300	*30.8	#10.05	*14.0
Famle	300	#5.14	#6.8	#4.56

** Significant at 0.01 level* *# Not significant at 0.01 level*

The chi-square values in Table 4.50 state that there was no significant association among environmental awareness, environmental attitude and environmental ethics of male and female teacher education students.

There was a positive significant association between environmental awareness and environmental attitude, environmental ethics and environmental awareness in male teacher education students and no significant association observed between environmental attitude and environmental ethics in male teacher education students.

In case of female teacher education students, there was no significant association between environmental awareness and environmental attitude, environmental attitude and environmental ethics and environmental ethics and environmental awareness.

The hypothesis that "There is no significant association among environmental awareness, environmental attitude and environmental ethics of male and female teacher education students" can be accepted as there is no significant association between environmental awareness and environmental attitude, environmental attitude and environmental ethics and environmental ethics and environmental awareness of male and female teacher education students, except in two cases in male teacher education students.

Hypothesis 4B

"There is no significant association among environmental awareness, environmental attitude and environmental ethics of rural and urban teacher education students".

The chi-square test was applied to test the validity of the hypothesis 4C.

Table 4.51
Association among Environmental Awareness, Environmental Attitude and Environmental Ethics of Rural and Urban Teacher Education Students

Variable	Sample Size	Environmental Awareness with Environmental Attitude	Environmental Attitude with Environmental Ethics	Environmental Ethics with Environmental Awareness
Rural	300	* 45.6	*81.2	#4.216
Urban	300	# 11.8	* 15.4	# 0.46

** Significant at 0.01 level* *# Not significant at 0.01 level*

The chi-square values in Table 4.51 state that there was both significant and not significant associations among environmental awareness, environmental attitude and environmental ethics of rural and urban teacher education students.

There was a positive significant association between environmental awareness and environmental attitude and environmental attitude and environmental ethics of rural teacher education students. There was no significant association between environmental awareness and environmental attitude of urban teacher education students.

There was no significant association between environmental ethics and environmental awareness of rural and urban teacher education students.

The hypothesis that "There is no significant association among environmental awareness, environmental attitude and environmental ethics of rural and urban teacher education students" can be rejected or accepted as equal number of associations were significant with regard to environmental awareness and environmental attitude and environmental attitude and environmental ethics and environmental ethics and environmental awareness in rural and urban teacher education students.

Hypothesis 4C

"There is no significant association among environmental awareness, environmental attitude and environmental ethics of science and arts teacher education students".

The chi-square test was applied to test the validity of the hypothesis 4C.

Table 4.52
Association among Environmental Awareness, Environmental Attitude and Environmental Ethic of Science and Arts Teacher Education Students

Variable	Sample Size	Environmental Awareness with Environmental Attitude	Environmental Attitude with Environmental Ethics	Environmental Ethics with Environmental Awareness
Science	300	#11.87	*28.19	#8.37
Arts	300	*26.5	*23.17	#0.617

** Significant at 0.01 level* *# Not significant at 0.01 level*

The chi-square values in Table 4.52 state that there was both significant and insignificant associations among environmental awareness, environmental attitude and environmental ethics of science and arts teacher education students.

There was no association between environmental awareness and environmental attitude and environmental awareness and environmental ethics of science teacher education students. There was a significant association between environmental ethics and environmental attitude of science teacher education students.

There was a significant association between environmental attitude and environmental awareness and environmental attitude and environmental ethics of arts teacher education students.

The hypothesis that "There is no significance association among environmental awareness, environmental attitude and environmental ethics of science and arts teacher education students" can be rejected or accepted as equal number of associations were significant and insignificant among environmental awareness, environmental attitude and environmental ethics of science and arts teacher education students.

Hypothesis 4D

"There is no significant association among environmental awareness, environmental attitude and environmental ethics of government and private college teacher education students".

The chi-square test was applied to test the validity of the hypothesis 4D.

Table 4.53

Association among Environmental Awareness, Environmental Attitude and Environmental Ethics of Government and Private College Teacher Education Students

Variable	Sample Size	Environmental Awareness with Environmental Attitude	Environmental Attitude with Environmental Ethics	Environmental Ethics with Environmental Awareness
Government	300	*37.06	*15.47	#10.12
Private	300	*29.81	62.89	#4.75

** Significant at 0.01 level* *# Not significant at 0.01 level*

The chi-square values in Table 4.53 reveal that there was both significant and insignificant associations among environmental awareness, environmental attitude and environmental ethics of government and private college teacher education students.

In the case of government teacher education students, there was a significant association between environmental awareness and environmental attitude, environmental attitude and environmental ethics, but no significant association between environmental ethics and environmental awareness.

In the case of private teachers education students, there was a significant association between environmental awareness and environmental attitude, environmental attitude and environmental ethics, though there was no significant association between environmental ethics and environmental awareness.

The hypothesis that "There is no significant association among environmental awareness, environmental attitude and environmental ethics of government and private college teacher education students" can be rejected as majority of the associations were significant.

Hypothesis 4E

"There is no significant association among environmental awareness, environmental attitude and environmental ethics of teacher education students with teaching experience and without teaching experience".

The chi-square test was applied to test the validity of the hypothesis 4E.

Table 4.54
Association among Environmental Awareness, Environmental Attitude and Environmental Ethics of Teacher Education Students with Teaching Experience and without Teaching Experience

Variable	Sample Size	Environmental Awareness with Environmental Attitude	Environmental Attitude with Environmental Ethics	Environmental Ethics with Environmental Awareness
Teaching experience	300	*25.00	*21.73	*16.32
No Teaching Experience	300	#3.57	#1.18	#7.78

** Significant at 0.01 level* *# Not significant at 0.01 level*

The chi-square values in Table 4.54 indicate that there was both significant and insignificant associations among environmental awareness, environmental attitude and environmental ethics of teacher education students with teaching experience and without teaching experience.

In the case of teacher education students with teaching experience, there was a significant association between environmental awareness and environmental attitude, environmental attitude and environmental ethics and environmental ethics and environmental awareness.

In the case of teacher education students without teaching experience, there was no significant association between environmental awareness and environmental attitude, environmental attitude and environmental ethics and environmental ethics and environmental awareness and they were independent of each other.

The hypothesis that "There is no significant association among environmental awareness, environmental attitude and environmental ethics of teacher education students with teaching and without teaching experience" can partly be accepted and partly be rejected as there was a significant association among environmental awareness, environmental attitude and environmental ethics of teacher education students with teaching experience and there was no significant association among environmental awareness, environmental attitude and environmental ethics of teacher education students without teaching experience.

Hypothesis 4F

"There is no significant association among environmental awareness, environmental attitude and environmental ethics of teacher education students aged below 25 years and above 25 years".

The chi-square test was applied to test the validity of the hypothesis 4F.

The chi-square values in Table 4.55 indicate that there was both significant and insignificant associations among environmental awareness, environmental attitude and environmental ethics of teacher education students aged below 25 years and above 25 years.

In the case of teacher education students aged below 25 years, there was a significant association between environmental

Table 4.55
Association among Environmental Awareness, Environmental Attitude and Environmental Ethics of Teacher Education Students Aged Below 25 Years and Above 25 Years

Variable	Sample Size	Environmental Awareness with Environmental Attitude	Environmental Attitude with Environmental Ethics	Environmental Ethics with Environmental Awareness
Aged below 25 years	300	*20.27	#5.48	#7.2
Aged above 25 years	300	#5.29	*14.18	#5.74

* *Significant at 0.01 level* # *Not significant at 0.01 level*

awareness and environmental attitude, whereas there was no significant association between environmental attitude and environmental ethics and environmental ethics and environmental awareness.

In the case of teacher education students aged above 25 years, there was a significant association between environmental attitude and environmental ethics, whereas there was no significant association between environmental awareness and environmental attitude and environmental ethics and environmental awareness.

The hypothesis that "there is no significant association among environmental awareness, environmental attitude and environmental ethics of teacher education students aged above 25 years and aged below 25 years" can be accepted as majority of the associations were insignificant.

Hypothesis 4G

"There is no significant association among environmental awareness environmental attitude and environmental ethics of B.Ed. and M.Ed. teacher education students".

The chi-square test was applied to test the validity of the hypothesis 4G.

Table 4.56
Association among Environmental Awareness Environmental Attitude and Environmental Ethic of B.Ed. and M.Ed. Teacher Education Students

Variable	Sample Size	Environmental Awareness with Environmental Attitude	Environmental Attitude with Environmental Ethics	Environmental Ethics with Environmental Awareness
B.Ed.	400	#1.95	*20.23	*23.0
M.Ed.	200	# 0.53	*27.94	*21.46

** Significant at 0.01 level* *# Not significant at 0.01 level*

The Chi-square values in Table 4.56 indicate there was both significant and insignificant associations among environmental awareness, environmental attitude and environmental ethics of B.Ed. and M.Ed. teacher education students.

In the case of B.Ed. teacher education students, there was no significant association between environmental awareness and environmental attitude, whereas there was significant association between environmental attitude and environmental ethics and environmental ethics and environmental awareness.

In the case of M.Ed. teacher education students, there was no significant association between environmental awareness and environmental attitude, whereas there was significant association between environmental attitude and environmental ethics and environmental ethics and environmental awareness.

There was no significant association between environmental awareness and environmental attitude in both B.Ed. and M.Ed. teacher education students and, hence, these traits can be considered as independent of each other.

The hypothesis that "There is no significant association among environmental awareness, environmental attitude and environmental ethics of B.Ed. and M.Ed. teacher education students" can be rejected as majority of associations were significant.

5

SUMMARY, CONCLUSIONS, DISCUSSION AND SUGGESTIONS

The summary, conclusions, discussions and suggestions are presented in this chapter.

SUMMARY

Teacher education students become future teachers and teacher educators. Their environmental awareness, environmental attitude and environmental ethics make them to introduce new methods, strategies and techniques of teaching environmental education for increasing student standards.

Environmental awareness is the sensitivity to the total environment and its allied problems. The development of environmental awareness means to understand the environmental problems and to develop critical thinking and problem solving skill in the people. Teachers can play a pivotal role in educating their students about environment, which is possible only when the teachers themselves have the necessary level of environmental awareness.

Environmental attitude is a set of values and feelings of concern for the environment and the motivation for active participation in environmental improvement and protection. The attitude of teachers can be changed by exposing them to recent developments in environmental issues.

Environmental ethics refers to the responsibility of understanding the environmental consequences of our consumption and need for recognising our responsibility to conserve natural resources and protect the earth for future generations. Environmental ethics education involves the teaching of cause and effect in a far-reaching scope, understanding environmental issues, means of understanding the long-term effects of decision-making.

The present study was intended to measure the environmental awareness, environmental attitude and environmental ethics of teacher education students and the association among environmental awareness, environmental attitude and environmental ethics.

The variables considered for the present study were gender, locality of teacher education college, subject of teacher education student (science and arts), management of teacher education college, teaching experience of teacher education student, age of teacher education student and qualification (B.Ed. and M.Ed.) of teacher education student. The present study was confined to the teacher education students of Hyderabad and Secunderabad twin cities and its surrounding rural areas.

The objectives considered for the present study were:

1. To find out the environmental awareness, environmental attitude and environmental ethics of teacher education students.
2. To find out the difference in the environmental awareness, environmental attitude and environmental ethics of male and female teacher education students.
3. To find out the difference in the environmental awareness, environmental attitude and environmental ethics of rural and urban teacher education students.
4. To find out the difference in the environmental awareness, environmental attitude and environmental ethics of science and arts teacher education students.
5. To find out the difference in the environmental awareness, environmental attitude and environmental ethics of government and private college teacher education students.

6. To find out the difference in the environmental awareness, environmental attitude and environmental ethics of teacher education students with teaching experience and without teaching experience.
7. To find out the difference in the environmental awareness, environmental attitude and environmental ethics of teacher education students aged below 25 years and above 25 years.
8. To find out the difference in the environmental awareness, environmental attitude and environmental ethics of B.Ed. and M.Ed. teacher education students.
9. To find out the association among environmental awareness, environmental attitude and environmental ethics of teacher education students.
10. To find out the association among environmental awareness, environmental attitude and environmental ethics of male and female teacher education students, rural and urban teacher education students, science and arts teacher education students, government and private college teacher education students, teacher education students with teaching experience and without teaching experience, teacher education students aged below 25 years, and above 25 years, and B.Ed. and M.Ed. teacher education students.

Rajput, Saxena and Jadhao (1980), Gupta (1981), Paramjeet (1993), Pradhan (1995), Magheda (1985), Dhiliwal (1985), Bains (1982), Comber and Keeves (1973), Seeni and Manickam (2002). Bapat and Rao (2004), Sebastian and Nima (2005), Nagra (2010), Pushpa (2010), Mondal (2011), Harjeet (2012) and Manpreet (2012) have conducted research on environmental awareness.

Jayantamete and Samaddar (2006), Shobeiri and Prahallada (2006), Kukreti (1993), Gupta and Prahara (1991), Kidwai (1991), Lahiri (2000), Kumar and Patil (2007), Patrick (1993), Saglam (2011) and Harjeet (2012) have conducted research on environmental attitude.

Rajiv (2007), Prasart (2009), Ondojuz (2009), Mehpare (2009), Suinn (2009), Suresh (2011) and Anjuli (2012) have conducted research on environmental ethics.

The normative survey method was used to study environmental awareness, environmental attitude and environmental ethics of teacher education students.

The variables, *viz.*, male *vs.* female teacher education students, rural versus urban teacher education students, science *vs.* arts teacher education students, government *vs.* private college teacher education students, teacher education students with teaching experience *vs.* without teaching experience, teacher education students aged below 25 years versus above 25 years, and B.Ed. *vs.* M.Ed. teacher education students were selected considering their role in determining the level of environmental awareness, environmental attitude and environmental ethics.

The hypotheses were formulated taking the objectives into consideration. The hypotheses formulated were in Null form. They were:

Hypothesis 1: The teacher education students are not possessing high environmental awareness.

Hypothesis 1A: There is no significant difference in the environmental awareness of male and female teacher education students.

Hypothesis 1B: There is no significant difference in the environmental awareness of rural and urban teacher education students.

Hypothesis 1C: There is no significant difference in the environmental awareness of science and arts teacher education students.

Hypothesis 1D: There is no significant difference in the environmental awareness of government and private college teacher education students.

Hypothesis 1E: There is no significant difference in the environmental awareness of teacher education students with teaching experience and without teaching experience.

Hypothesis 1F: There is no significant difference in the environmental awareness of teacher education students aged below 25 years and aged above 25 years.

Hypothesis 1G: There is no significant difference in the environmental awareness of B.Ed. and M.Ed. teacher education students.

Hypothesis 2: The teacher education students are not possessing high environmental attitude.

Hypothesis 2A: There is no significant difference in the environmental attitude of male and female teacher education students.

Hypothesis 2B: There is no significant difference in the environmental attitude of rural and urban teacher education students.

Hypothesis 2C: There is no significant difference in the environmental attitude of science and arts teacher education students.

Hypothesis 2D: There is no significant difference in the environmental attitude of government and private college teacher education students.

Hypothesis 2E: There is no significant difference in the environmental attitude of teacher education students with teaching experience and without teaching experience.

Hypothesis 2F: There is no significant difference in the environmental attitude of teacher education students aged below 25 years and above 25 years.

Hypothesis 2G: There is no significant difference in the environmental attitude of B.Ed. and M.Ed. teacher education students.

Hypothesis 3: The teacher education students are not possessing high environmental ethics.

Hypothesis 3A: There is no significant difference in the environmental ethics of male and female teacher education students.

Hypothesis 3B: There is no significant difference in the environmental ethics of rural and urban teacher education students.

Hypothesis 3C: There is no significant difference in the environmental ethics of science and arts teacher education students.

Hypothesis 3D: There is no significant difference in the environmental ethics of government and private college teacher education students.

Hypothesis 3E: There is no significant difference in the environmental ethics of teacher education students with teaching experience and without teaching experience.

Hypothesis 3F: There is no significant difference in the environmental ethics of teacher education students aged below 25 years and above 25 years.

Hypothesis 3G: There is no significant difference in the environmental ethics of B.Ed. and M.Ed. teacher education students.

Hypothesis 4: There is no significant association among environmental awareness, environmental attitude and environmental ethics of teacher education students.

Hypothesis 4A: There is no significant association among environmental awareness, environmental attitude and environmental ethics of male and female teacher education students.

Hypothesis 4B: There is no significant association among environmental awareness, environmental attitude and environmental ethics of rural and urban teacher education students.

Hypothesis 4C: There is no significant association among environmental awareness, environmental attitude and environmental ethics of science and arts teacher education students.

Hypothesis 4D: There is no significant association among environmental awareness, environmental attitude and environmental ethics of government and private college teacher education students.

Hypothesis 4E: There is no significant association among environmental awareness, environmental attitude and environmental ethics of teacher education students with teaching experience and without teaching experience.

Hypothesis 4F: There is no significant association among environmental awareness, environmental attitude and environmental ethics of teacher education students aged below 25 years and above 25 years.

Hypothesis 4G: There is no significant association among environmental awareness, environmental attitude and environmental ethics of B.Ed. and M.Ed. teacher education students.

The stratified sampling technique was found appropriate for the present study because the present study involved in splitting the sample into a good number of groups according to different variables. Through stratified sampling only it is possible to divide the sample into different groups and choose teacher education students from each of these groups. Random sampling technique was also used to select the teacher education students from each group.

Regarding the size of the sample, 600 teacher education students were found to be appropriate. This was found suitable because the study involves due intensity and detail. Out of the total sample, when divided variable-wise, the size of the sample is 300 male teacher education students, 300 female teacher education students, 300 rural teacher education students, 300 urban teacher education students, 300 science teacher education students, 300 arts teacher education students, 300 government college teacher education students, 300 private college teacher education students, 300 teacher education students with teaching experience, 300 teacher education students without teaching experience, 300 teacher education students aged below 25 years, 300 teacher education students aged above 25 years, 400 B.Ed. teacher education students, 200 M.Ed. teacher education students.

The tools occupy a major role in any research because they are useful in the collection and analysis of data to draw meaningful conclusions. As the present study was an intensive one, the available standardized tools were selected.

Environmental Awareness Ability Measure (EAAM) developed by Praveen Kumar Jha (1998) was used to measure the environmental awareness of teacher education students. The investigator used the Taj Environmental Attitude Scale (TEAS) standardized by Haseen Taj to study the environmental attitude of teacher education students. Environmental Ethics Scale (EES) standardized by Haseen Taj was used to study the environmental ethics of teacher education students.

The mean, standard deviation, Critical ratio and Chi-square test were used to analyse the raw scores and to extract the findings. Based on the findings, suitable conclusions were drawn for necessary discussion and implementation.

CONCLUSIONS, DISCUSSION AND SUGGESTIONS

The following are the conclusions drawn from the analysis of data, and these are followed by necessary discussion and suggestions.

ENVIRONMENTAL AWARENESS OF TEACHER EDUCATION STUDENTS

1. **Teacher education students had average environmental awareness.**

This result was supported by Selvam and Boopalrajan (2003), Dharma Raja (2003), Abraham and Arjunan (2005), Manpreet Kaur (2012) and Amrit Paul Kaur and Mahabir Singh Bhatti (2012).

Teacher education colleges are the right places to play a right kind of role to imbibe the quality components of environment. There are some constraints while imparting environmental education through our teaching-learning process like:

(a) methods are theoretical ignoring the psychomotor domain;

(b) lack of necessary resource materials in teacher education colleges to improve the awareness.

The teacher education colleges should incorporate the environmental education in their academic activities and develop environmental awareness in their clientele to an optimum level.

2. **Male and female teacher education students had average environmental awareness without any significant difference between them.**

Garma Darshan (1996) and Maryam Larijani (2008) found that male teacher education students had more environmental awareness. Vipinder Nagra (2010), Ajay Kumar (2010), Pushpa Latha (2010) and Bhim Chandra Mondal (2011) supported the findings of the present study.

The present study tells that the impact of gender on environmental awareness and behaviour is not noticeable. The teacher education students, irrespective of their gender, should develop better environmental awareness and promote environmental tranquility.

3. **The rural and urban teacher education students had average environmental awareness with a significant difference between them. The urban teacher education students had better environmental awareness than their rural counterparts.**

Hampel, *et al.* (1995), Abraham and Nair (1998), Pushpa Latha (2010), Rao, (2010), Nagra and Dhillon (2006), Astalin (2008), Abraham and Arjunan (2005) reported a higher environmental awareness in urban population compared to rural subjects.

Urban teacher education students possessed more favorable awareness when compared to rural teachers. The reason for this is the extent of exposure to environmental issues and this exposure may be through electronic media and print media. Urban teacher education students are aware of various environmental programmes by the use of new technology inputs like multimedia and web based e-content programmes.

The rural teacher education students need to be on par with their urban counterparts and do participate in environmental activities and acquire required environmental awareness.

4. **The science and arts teacher education students had average environmental awareness with a significant difference between them. The science teacher education students had better environmental awareness than their arts counterparts.**

This study was supported by the studies of Bhattacharya (1977), Shabina (1999), Balkobi and Hadipour (2001), Pradhan (2002), Shaila (2003) and Vipinder and Jaswinder (2005). In opposition to these findings, Vinpinder (2010), Manpreet (2012), Ajay Kumar (2010) and Pushpa Latha (2010) found no significant difference in the subject of teacher education students.

Irrespective of subject disciplines, the activities that create environmental awareness in teacher education students include:

(a) campus greening;
(b) campus cleaning;
(c) field visits to places like forest ecology, marine ecology, terrestrial ecology;
(d) celebration of environment related days;
(e) competitions in institutions;
(f) mini exhibitions; and
(g) use of audio visual materials.

5. **Government and private college teacher education students had average environmental awareness without any significant difference between them.**

This finding was supported by Pushpa Latha (2010).

Government of India is taking initiation with the collaboration of Ministry of Environment and Forests and Department of education of Ministry of Human Resource Development for the expansion of environmental education and its proper place in teacher education programmes, which will sensitize the teacher education institutions on issues related campaigns to be initiated at local and government level to involve them in environmental protection programmes. UGC is using the television networks to take high quality environmental films to remote areas. Government should also introduce environmental education as a compulsory subject in various teacher education curricula. Teacher education colleges should have flexible curriculum to acquaint the students with environmental issues and concerns.

6. **Teacher education students with and without teaching experience had average environmental awareness with a significant difference between them. Teacher education students with teaching experience had better environmental awareness than teacher education students without teaching experience.**

Peal (1995) reported that the experience of teachers did not play an important role on environmental awareness. Shobeiri (2007) observed that the length of teaching experience had impact on gaining environmental awareness.

Irrespective of the teaching experience, all the teacher education students should acquire environmental awareness in order to have a good environment in and around educational institutions.

7. **Teacher education students aged below 25 years and above 25 years had average environmental awareness with a significant difference between them. Teacher education students aged above 25 years had better environmental awareness than teacher education students aged below 25 years.**

Larijani (2008) earlier found that the teacher education students with more age had higher level of environmental awareness.

With the age, the teacher education students gain maturity and develop critical thinking to understand the nature and scope of various environmental problems. To create environmental awareness among teacher education students and to promote responsible environmental behaviour, more extracurricular activities need to be provided by organizing workshops, playing, plays, showing movies and forming of environmental clubs in teacher education colleges.

8. **B.Ed. and M.Ed. teacher education students had average environmental awareness with a significant difference between them. B.Ed. teacher education students had better environmental awareness than M.Ed. teacher education students.**

This study was supported by the findings of Selvam and Booparajan (2003), Harjeet Kaur (2012), Manpreet Kaur (2012) and Amritpal Kaur and Mahavir Singh (2012).

Co-curricular projects and life skill projects need be employed for creating environmental awareness among teacher education students. In teacher education colleges, there is a need to develop and display the environmental education materials like posters, models, films, stories, charts, manuals in local languages.

ENVIRONMENTAL ATTITUDE OF TEACHER EDUCATION STUDENTS

9. Teacher education students had high environmental attitude.

The studies of Kuhlemeier, *et al.* (1999), Kandir, Adalet, Yurt and Kalburan (2012), Kumar and Patil (2007) and Mahbub Sarkar (2007) supported this finding.

There is a need for the professional development of all teachers in environmental concepts to develop students as most precious resources for protecting the environment. Teachers can play an important role in educating their students about environment, which is possible only when teachers themselves have the necessary level of environmental attitude. Teacher education courses need be enriched by introducing environmental activities, starting ecoclubs, celebrating environmental days and taking up projects related to environmental problems as these develop a positive attitude towards preservation and protection of environment.

10. Male and female teacher education students had high environmental attitude with a significant difference between them. Female teacher education students had better environmental attitude than male teacher education students.

Sabhlok (1995), Mahbub Sarkar (2011) and Shabeiri, *et al.* (2006) noticed that male and female teacher education students significantly differ in their environmental attitude and female teacher education students had more environmental attitude. But, Hart and Naolan (1992) and Abraham and Nair (1998) observed that male teachers possessed better attitude towards environment compared to female prospective teachers. Shaila (2003) indicated that the gender had no effect on environmental attitude.

The teacher education students, irrespective of their gender, need to develop a better attitude towards environment, so that the environment of the viscinity is saved and improved.

11. **Rural and urban teacher education students had high environmental attitude with a significant difference between them. Urban teacher education students had better environmental attitude than rural teacher education students.**

The finding that the urban teacher education students possessed better attitude towards environment compared to their rural counterparts was supported by Hampel, *et al.* (1995), Abraham and Nair (1998), Dinakara (2000), Shaila (2003), Roll (1995) and Mahbub Sarkar (2011).

This high attitude may be because urban teacher education students are confronted with more environmental problems such as pollution, water scarecity, over population and urban congestion that include higher levels of environmental concerns.

Both rural and urban teacher education students should have a better environmental attitude in order to live and lead a happy life in an eco-friendly environment.

12. **Science and arts teacher education students had high environmental attitude with a significant difference between them. Science teacher education students had better environmental attitude than arts teacher education students.**

Bhattacharya (1977), Kumar and Patil (2007), Sudheshna Lahiri (2010) and Harjeet Kaaur (2012) noticed that science teacher education students possessed better environmental attitude than arts teacher education students.

Participation in activities to save the environment, prevention of pollution, being aware of environmental issues, saving greenary, developing higher environmental attitude helps in developing higher environmental attitude.

The teacher education students, without much botheration about their place of living, need to develop better environmental attitude to live comfortably.

13. **Government and private college teacher education students had high environmental attitude without any significant difference between them.**

The key to environmental education lies with teachers, and hence the government should introduce and enrich environmental education programmes in the teacher education institutions. The agencies like DIETs, SCERTs, State pollution control boards, NCTE, UGC, NCERT, etc., should organize, from time to time, seminars, conferences, workshops, refresher courses, etc., in teacher education colleges. Environmental journals need be made available in all teacher education institutions. All these will help teacher education students to inculcate proper environmental attitude.

14. **Teacher education students with and without teaching experience had high environmental attitude with a significant difference between them. Teacher education students with teaching experience had better environmental attitude than teacher education students without any teaching experience.**

Kellner and Waupinski (1974) and International Network (2005) found that teaching experience has significantly influenced to have more environmental attitude.

By working with the administrations and faculties of teacher education institutions with rich experience, we can bring effective change in teaching learning process, which could reorient the behaviour of teacher education students and shape up future generations.

15. **Teacher education students aged below 25 years and above 25 years had high environmental attitude without any significant difference between them.**

Ahlberg and Filho (1998) noticed that environmental attitude can be enhanced by teaching material irrespective of the age of the students.

Tutorial support, live experiments, field work, policying the goals and methods to be used in linking formal and informal education, community involvement, interest, networking, efforts to extend learning opportunities, use of mass media, curricular contents, teaching strategies, instructional devices are to be judiciously implemented in the teacher education colleges to develop better environmental attitude.

16. B.Ed. and M.Ed. teacher education students had high environmental attitude with a significant difference between them. M.Ed. teacher education students had better environmental attitude than B.Ed. teacher education students.

Braus (1995), Myburg (1994), Shongwe (1992) and Simmon (1993) observed that teachers lack the necessary skills, knowledge and attitude to teach about environment. Hurry (1982) noticed that environmental concepts never received strong emphasis in pre-service and in-service teacher education. Kuiper (1995) and Kandir, Adalet, Yurt and Kalburan (2012) found that there are not enough number of teachers trained in environmental education.

The teacher education colleges need to provide necessary knowledge and skills to develop better environmental attitude in their student teachers.

ENVIRONMENTAL ETHICS OF TEACHER EDUCATION STUDENT

17. Teacher education students had average environmental ethics.

Studies of Roth (1992), Lundmark (2007), Yaikaew (2007), Jueprasit (2005) and Jatupornpong (2005) supported the finding of their study.

Anjuli Suhani (2012) found high environmental ethics among teacher education students.

There is a need to develop environmental ethics among teacher education students to bear a responsibility of propagating environmental ideas, developing understanding about environment and deepening ideas of environmental issues and to improve the skills by teachers and teacher educators of respective institutions. As environmental ethics develops collaborative thinking, manifold and holistic thinking, critical thinking, analytical reasoning and communication in the community, the teacher education students can share their ideas and can listen and respond to each other in the society. So, teacher education students should develop better environmental ethics.

18. Male and female teacher education students had average environmental ethics without any significant difference between them.

Mellor (2006), Partridge (1995), Kaewnum (2005), Thana Sathit (2004) and Anjuli Suhane (2012) have claimed that domination of nature by women is more. Females have moral/political calling to renew the world or heal the wounds of an ecologically destructive socio-economic order. Therefore, education authorities should implement environmental ethics education, which aims at behavioural concern towards environment in teacher education institutions.

19. Rural and urban teacher education students had average environmental ethics with a significant difference between them. Urban teacher education students had better environmental ethics than rural teacher education students.

Nuangchalerm and Prachagool (2010) supported the above finding.

Suresh Kotwani (2011) found no significant difference between rural and urban teacher education students with regard to environmental ethics.

Urban environmental problems are mainly concerned to two important issues – over consumption and over population. The quality of life of people living in urban areas has declined because of pollution, over crowding of people and scarcity of resources. Protection of the environment is one of the major challenges the urban world as well as rural world is facing. Teachers should know which objects to be reduced, reversed and recycled in our environment. Teacher education institutions alone are the powerful media to ensure environmental protection. Environmental ethics are very much important for the teachers and teacher educators as they can transform the culture of consumption of natural resources and generation of sustainable environment based life styles and communities based on environmental needs rather than wants.

20. Science and arts teacher education students had average environmental ethics with a significant difference between them. Science teacher education students had better environmental ethics than arts teacher education students.

Anjuli Suhane (2012) found no significant difference of environmental ethics with course subject.

After class 10th, the arts curriculum does not give much importance to environmental concepts except the dimensions such as population, forests, etc., where as science students are exposed continuously to conceptual awareness of environmental issues. Hence, the teacher education students of all subjects need to be made aware of environment to promote environmental ethics in them.

21. Government and private college teacher education students had average environmental ethics without any significant difference between them.

The study of Suresh and Kotwani (2011) supported the above finding.

National Symposium on Environmental Ethics (March 1992, New Delhi held in collaboration with UNESCO-UNEP) suggested that ethics is an internalized code of behaviour that helps to create a social order which protects nature and basic human rights; at the same time, capable of integrating economy and ecology, material and ethical progress, science and spirituality. What the teachers and teacher educators do to their environment depends on their values. Hence, teacher education institutions should inculcate environmental ethics through curricula or projects suitable for sustainable development of the environment.

22. Teacher education students with and without teaching experience had average environmental ethics without any significant difference between them.

Sake, Surmeli and Oztuna (2009) and Anjuli Suhane (2012) found that pre-service teachers who participated in an environmental course had higher level of ecocentric concern.

Teacher education institutions could play a major role in imparting ethics by educating pre-service teachers and by updating their environmental knowledge and skills. The teacher education curriculum may also provide programmes for the professional development of pre-service teachers. Then they may have concern and positive thinking for preserving and conserving the environment and also carefully act in using environment-friendly products.

23. **Teacher education students aged below 25 years and above 25 years had average environmental ethics without any significant difference between them.**

Partridge (1995) noticed that environmental values are evoked, not by age, but by personal appreciation of nature.

Irrespective of age, human beings should have aesthetic sense of natural environment to develop environmental ethics, which involve examination of current beliefs, changing beliefs and their effect on environmental values. So, the teacher education students should have better environmental ethics.

24. **B.Ed. and M.Ed. teacher education students had average environmental ethics with a significant difference between them. B.Ed. teacher education students had better environmental ethics than M.Ed. teacher education students.**

The study of Anjuli Suhane (2012) supported the present finding.

Environmental ethics are based on a commitment to shape the world in which we live through thoughtful and active participation. It calls for a perspective that acknowledges that each of our actions has an effect in entire global system. Teacher education institutions should make the student teachers to explore how cultural, social and political organizations and the stages of development of groups of people contribute to environmental effects, explore ethical issues involved in environmental protection and management issues in scientific, economic, legal, social and political context and on education.

ASSOCIATION AMONG ENVIRONMENTAL AWARENESS, ENVIRONMENTAL ATTITUDE AND ENVIRONMENTAL ETHICS OF TEACHER EDUCATION STUDENTS

25. **There was a significant association between environmental attitude and environmental ethics and environmental ethics**

and environmental awareness of teacher education students. There was no significant association between environmental awareness and environmental attitude of teacher education students.

The studies of Lundmark (2007), Chawla and Cushing (2007), Sadler (2004), Sadler and Zeidler (2005), Matkins and Bell (2007), Nuangchalerm (2009), Palmer (1998), Kennedy, *et al*. (2009) supported the present finding.

Teacher education institutions should provide the educational programmes that may equip the teacher education students with techniques and strategies that inculcate right attitude towards environment and awareness of environment and environmental ethics.

26. **There was a significant association between environmental awareness and environmental attitude and environmental attitude and environmental awareness, but there was no significant association between environmental attitude and environmental ethics of male teacher education students. There was no significant association between environmental awareness and environmental attitude and environmental attitude and environmental ethics and environmental ethics and environmental awareness of female teacher education students.**

The teacher education students should be aware of various environmental aspects so as to develop attitude, awareness and ethics concerned to environment to be a part in sustainable development of environment.

27. **There was a significant association between environmental awareness and environmental attitude and environmental attitude and environmental ethics and there was no significant association between environmental ethics and environmental awareness of rural teacher education students. There was no significant association between environmental awareness and environmental attitude and environmental awareness and environmental ethics and a significant association between environmental ethics and environmental attitude of urban teacher education students.**

There is a need for better environmental awareness, environmental attitude and environmental ethics among teacher education students so that they may become part and parcel of the vicinity's environment.

28. **There was no significant association between environmental awareness and environmental attitude and environmental awareness and environmental ethics, but there was a significant association between environmental ethics and environmental attitude of science teacher education students. There was a significant association between environmental awareness and environmental attitude and environmental attitude and environmental ethics, but there was no significant association between environmental ethics and environmental awareness of arts teacher education students.**

Teacher education students by possessing a right attitude, better awareness and useful ethics concerned to environment may help the environment become friendly to human life and living.

29. **There was a significant association between environmental awareness and environmental attitude and environmental attitude and environmental ethics and environmental ethics but there was no significant association between environmental awareness of government college teacher education students. There was a significant association between environmental awareness and environmental attitude and environmental attitude and environmental ethics, but there was no significant association between environmental ethics and environmental awareness of private college teacher education students.**

The teacher education students with better environmental awareness, attitude and ethics can do their best for the benefit of local as well as remote environment, which in turn get benefit out of better environment.

30. **There was a significant association among environmental awareness, environmental attitude and environmental ethics of teacher education students with teaching experience and there was no significant association among environmental**

awareness, environmental attitude and environmental ethics of teacher education students without any teaching experience.

The teacher education students with or without teaching experience, by having expectable levels of environmental awareness, attitude and ethics, may modify the environment to meet the needs and necessities of mankind.

31. **There was a significant association between environmental awareness and environmental attitude, but there was no significant association between environmental attitude and environmental ethics and environmental ethics and environmental awareness of teacher education students aged below 25 years. There was a significant association between environmental attitude and environmental ethics, but there was no significant association between environmental awareness and environmental attitude and environmental ethics and environmental awareness of teacher education students aged above 25 years.**

The teacher education students with proper environmental awareness, attitude and ethics may change the climate of the environment in which they live, learn and earn.

32. **There was a significant association between environmental attitude and environmental ethics and environmental ethics and environmental awareness, but there was no significant association between environmental awareness and environmental attitude of B.Ed. teacher education students. There was a significant association between environmental attitude and environmental ethics and environmental ethics and environmental awareness, but there was no significant association between environmental awareness and environmental attitude of M.Ed. teacher education students.**

The teacher education students through first-hand experiences of environment will gain environmental awareness, attitude and ethics and help, along with them, others in participating in sustainable development of friendly environment.

SUGGESTIONS FOR FURTHER RESEARCH

In the light of the present study, the following studies may be taken up by the researchers.

1. A study on environmental awareness of students from various standards can be conducted.
2. A study on environmental awareness of parents of students can be conducted.
3. A study on environmental awareness of teachers at different levels can be conducted.
4. The content on the environmental education in the text books can be analyzed.
5. An investigation on environmental dimensions can be carried out at different district levels.
6. A study on the relationship between knowledge and awareness on environment can be conducted.
7. A study on exploration of determinants of environmentally responsible behaviour and its influence on environmental literature can be conducted.
8. A study on environmental attitude of students of different stages of education can be done.
9. A study on development of environmental literacy for prospective teachers can be done.
10. A study on environmental knowledge, environmental attitude and perception regarding environmental education among pre-service and in-service school teachers can be done.
11. A study on academic avenues through e-learning for environmental awareness can be studied.
12. A study on environmental attitude and pro-environmental behaviour among teachers can be done.
13. A study on environmental ethics and process of thinking among teachers can be conducted.
14. A study on environmental attitude, behaviour and ethics of elementary school students can be done.
15. A study on challenges of cross cultural ethics for environmental protection can be done.

BIBLIOGRAPHY

Aggarwal, S.K. and Garg , R.K. (1988), *Environment Issues and Research in India*. Udaipur: Himanshi Publications.

Aggarwal, Y.P. (1988), *Research in Emerging Fields of Education – Concepts, Trends and Prospects*. New Delhi: Sterling Publishers Pvt. Ltd., New Delhi.

Ahluwallis, S.P. and Bais, H.S. (1993), *Issues and Challenges*. New Delhi: Ashish Publishing House.

Ambasht, R.S. and Ambasht, P.K. (1994), *Environmental and Pollution – An Ecological Approach*. Varanasi: Friends Co.

Abraham, M. and Arjunan, N.K. (2005), Environmental Attitude and Pro-environmental Behaviour among Secondary School Children. *Edutracks*, 4(6), 32-34.

Aminuddi Hasan, Hafizan Juahir and Nur Syuhada Jamaludin (2009), The Level of Environmental Awareness among Students to Fulfill the Aspiration of National Philosophy of Education. *American Journal of Scientific Research*, 223(5), 50-58.

Arumugarajan, R. (2010), Environmental Awareness of IXth Std Students in Tuticorin District. *Edutracks*, 10(2), 23-26.

Antony Brock (1978), Environmental Education. *Educational Review*, 84(6), 81-85.

Amritpal Kaur and Mahabir Singh Bhati (2012), Environmental Education in Teacher Education. *Indian Streams Research Journal*, 49(20), 231-251.

Atkinson, J. Berne, E. and Woodworth, R.S. (1996), *Dictionary of Psychology*. New Delhi: Goyal Saab Publishers and Distributors.

Buch, M.B. (Ed.) (1978), *Second Survey of Research in Education*. Baroda: CASE.

Buch, M.B. (Ed.) (1987), *Third Survey of Research in Education*. New Delhi: NCERT.

Buch, M.B. (Ed.) (1991), *Fourth Survey of Research in Education*. New Delhi: NCERT.

Badkobi, A. and Hadipour, M. (2001), Assessment of Primary School Teachers Educational Condition in Different Zones of Tehran Municipality in Environmental Subjects and the ways of Elevating their Awareness. *Scientific Quarterly Journal of Environment*, 33, 79-80.

Bahrainy, H. and Amini, F. (2001), The Role of Environmental Non-governmental Organization in Citizens Participation for Environmental Conservation in Iran. *Journal of Environmental Studies*, 26, 4-12.

Best, John W. (1982), *Research in Education* (4th ed.). New Delhi: Prentice Hall of India Pvt. Ltd.

Best, John W. (2003), *Research in Education* (9th ed.). New Delhi: Prentice Hall of India Pvt. Ltd.

Balamurugan, G. (2005), *A Study on the Environmental Awareness among XIth Standard Students in Different Types of Schools in Theni District*. M.Ed. Dissertation, Department of Education, Madras University.

Bhattacharya, N. (2003), *A Critical Analysis of Environmental Education Curriculum for Prospective Teachers*. Paper Presented in the National Seminar on 36th Annual Conference, Uttaranchal, IATE.

Bhim Chandra, Mondal (2010), A Comparative Study of Environmental Awareness among Secondary School Students in Relation to Gender and Residential Background. *Sikshachintan*, 4, 17-20.

Bhargava, G. (1992), *Pollution and Its Control*. New Delhi: Ashish Publication House.

Bhaskara Rao, Digumarti (2004), *Methods of Teaching Environmental Science*. New Delhi: Discovery Publishing House. ISBN 81-7141-893-2.

Chethana, S. (2003), Effect of Background Variables on the Environmental Attitude of 9th Standard Students. M.A. Dissertation, Department of Studies and Research Education, Karnataka State Open University, Mysore. 131-153.

Chandrasekhar, (2008), *Environmental Awareness among 10th Class Students of Hyderabad City*. Quest in Education Vol. XXXII No. 1 pp. 6-11.

Chandini Saxena, (2006), Environmental Awareness in Ancient India. *University New Journal*, Vol. 44, No. 12, March 20-26, p. 79-84.

Chandy, K.T. (1991). Environmental Awareness. *Legal News and Views*, 5, 2-9.

Deb, S.K. (2006), Perspective on Environmental Education: Challenge to Civilization. *Edutracks*, 6(3), 9-11.

Dinakara, S.A. (2000), *Environmental Awareness, Environmental Attitude and Teaching Practices of Elementary School Teachers of Mysore District in Environmental Related Topics*. M.Ed. Dissertation, Department of Education, Mysore University.

Dunlap, R.E. (1994), International Attitude Towards Environment and Development. *Green Globe Year Book of International Co-operation*, 4(5), 115-126.

Darshan, Garima (1997), *A Study of Environmental Component in the Text Book of CBSE in Generating Environmental Awareness among Students*. M.Ed Dissertation, Department of Education, Rohelkhand University.

Durga Malathi, K. (2002), *A Study on the Environmental Awareness among IXth Standard Students*. M.Ed. Dissertation, Department of Education, Madras University.

David. G. Victor (2004), *Climate Change – Debating Americans Policy Optimas*, Council in Foreign Realtors Press, New York.

Deb, S.K. and Bhattacharya, N. (2006), Prospective on Environment Education Challenge to Civilization. *Edutracks,* 6(3), 11-14.

Daniel, J. (2007), *Education for Sustainable Development: Reaching the Masses.* Ahmedabad: Fourth International Conference on Environmental Education.

Ediger, Marlow and Rao, Digumarti Bhaskara (2005), *Teaching Science in Elementary Schools.* New Delhi: Discovery Publishing House.

Fisher, R.A. (1950), *Statistical Methods for Research Workers.* New York: Hafner Publishing Co.

Fien, J. and Tilbury, D. (1997), *Learning for A Sustainable Environment: An Agenda for Teacher Education in Asia and Pacific.* Bangkok: UNESCO-ACEID.

Garrett, H. E. (1973), *Statistics in Psychology and Education.* Bombay: Vikas, Feffer and Simon Pvt. Ltd.

Gayford, C. (1987), Training and Education in Relation to Environmental Problems. *Annual Review of Environmental Education,* 1, 10-12.

Greenall, A. (1981), Environmental Education: A Case Study in National Curriculum Action. *International Journal of Environmental Education and Information,* 1(4), 285-294.

Grendstand, G. (1998), The Effect of Values, Beliefs and Personal Norms on Environmental Behaviour of Children. *Journal of social Issues,* 57, 19-34.

Gupta, V.S. (1987), Environmental Awareness and Mass Media. *Vidura,* 24(1), 112-116.

Gnanadevan, R. (2007), Environmental Awareness of Higher Secondary Students. *Research and Reflection on Education,* 5(1), 9-11.

Gihar, S., Saxena, M.K. and Kukreti, B.R. (2006), Developing Environmental-friendly Behaviour among Students: Role of Video Intervention. *University News,* 44(12), 69-74.

Hungerford, H., Peyton, R.B. and Wilke, R.J. (1980), Goals for Curriculum Development in Environmental Education. *Journal of Environmental Education,* 11(3), 42-47.

Hyland, T. (1993), Competence and Competencies. *Journal of Philosophy of Education*, 27(1), 57-68.

Haseen, Taj (2001), *Manual for Environmental Attitude Scale*. Agra: Nandini Enterprises.

Henry, E. (1981), *Statistics in Psychology and Education*. Bombay: Vaklis, Feffer and Simans Ltd.

Hampel, B. Holdswroth, R. and Boldero, J. (1995), Urban Rural Difference in Environmental Consciousness among Adolescents. *Draft of Rural Society*, 5(4), 78-86.

Haseen, Taj (2001), *Manual for Environmental Ethics Scale*. Agra: Nandini Enterprises.

Jensen, B.B. and Schnack, K. (1997), The Action Competence Approach in Environmental Education. *Environmental Education Research*, 3(2), 163-178.

Jinarajan, S. (1999), *A Study of Environmental Awareness and Attitude Towards Environmental Education of Student Teachers of Bangalore City*. M.Phil Dissertation. Department of Education, Bangalore University.

Jayanta, Mete and Parama Samaddar (2006), Development and Implementation of Environmental Education Curriculum for Secondary Schools: The Indian Context. *Perspectives in Education*, 22(1), 41-48.

Jadhar, H.V. (1996), *A Text Book of Environmental Science Education*. New Delhi: Sterling Publishers Pvt. Ltd.

John, Fien and Daniella, Tilbury (1996), *Learning for a Sustainable Environment: An Agenda for Teacher Education in Asia and the Pacific*. Thailand: UNESCO.

Krishnamacharyulu, V. and Reddy, G.S. (2005), *Environmental Education Aims and Objectives of Environmental Education: Importance of Environmental Education*. Hyderabad: Neelkamal Publication Pvt. Ltd.

Kuldeep Singh, Katoch (2001), Environmental Awareness and Attitude of Teachers of Himachal Pradesh. *University News*, 48(23), 21-41.

Kaushik and Kaushik, A.K. (2009), *Perspective in Environmental Studies*. New Delhi: New Age International Pvt. Ltd.

Kukreti, B.R. (1993), Environmental Education: A Blue Print. *University News*, 31(33), 11-19.

Kuhlemeir, H., Bergh, H.V.D. and Lagerweij, N. (1999), Environmental Knowledge, Attitude and Behaviour Dutch Secondary Education. *Journal of Environmental Education*, 30(2), 4-14.

Kaimi, D. (2003), A Survey on Environmental Education Needs for Students, Teachers and Housewives in the Khak Sefid District of Tehran, *Scientific Quarterly Journal of Environment*, 40, 80-90.

Kaur Amandeep, *et al.* (2006), *Environmental Education.* Ludhiana: Tandon Publications.

Khoshoo, T.N. (1991), *Environmental Concerns and Strategies.* New Delhi: Ashish Publishing House.

Kothari, D.S. (1966), *Report of the Education Commission,* 1964-66. New Delhi: Government of India.

Lederman, N.G. (1992), Students' and Teachers' Conceptions of the Nature of Science: A Review of the Research, *Journal of Research in Science Teaching,* 29, 331-359.

Mudaliar, A.L. (1953), *Report of the Secondary Education Commission, 1952-53.* New Delhi: Government of India.

Mary Sahaya, R. and Paul Raj, I. (2005), Environmental Awareness Among High School Students. *Edutracks,* 5(4), 33-35.

Mangal, S.K. (2002), *Statistics in Psychology and Education.* New Delhi: Prentice-Hall of India Pvt. Ltd.

Mangal, S.K. and Uma, Mangal (2009), *Essentials of Educational Technology.* New Delhi: PHI Learning Private Limited.

Mercy, A. and Arjunan, N.K. (2005), Environmental Attitude and Pro-environmental Behaviour among Secondary School Children. *Edutracks,* 4(6), 32-34.

Mourya, K. and Ashwani, G. (1997), *A Study to Observe Awareness on Environment and Energy Resources amongs Tharu Students,* M.Ed Dissertation, Department of Education, Rohelkhand University.

Modi, V. (2005), Environmental Education and Teacher. *Bharateeya Shikshan,* 15(7), 14-16.

Mustafa, Metin, Kerem, Coskun and Yavuz, Topkaya (2011), Are the Primary Pre-service Teachers Aware of Environmental Problems, *World Applied Sciences Journal,* 13 (3), 396-403.

Mishra, A., Mallik, U., Gill, J., Sinha, S. and Lahiry, D. (1985), *Environmental Education Pre-service Teacher Training Curriculum Development.* Unpublished Document Presented to UNESCO.

NCERT (1997), *Fifth Survey of Research in Education (1988-1992) – Trend Reports, Volume – I.* New Delhi: National Council for Educational Research and Training.

NCERT (1997), *Fifth Survey of Research in Education, (1988-1992) – Research Abstracts, Volume – II.* New Delhi: National Council for Educational Research and Training.

NCERT (1978), *Teacher Education Curriculum: A Framework Prepared for National Council for Teacher Education.* New Delhi: NCERT.

NCTE (2007), *Curriculum Framework: Teacher Education for A Knowledge Society (Draft).* New Delhi: NCTE.

NCTE (2008), *Teacher Education Curriculum: Bases and Frameworks (Draft).* New Delhi: NCTE.

NCTE (2009a), *National Curriculum Framework for Teacher Education 2009.* New Delhi: NCTE.

NCTE (2009b), *National Curriculum Framework for Teacher Education: Towards Preparing Professional and Humane Teacher.* New Delhi: NCTE.

NCTE-NCERT (2006), *Curriculum Framework for Teacher Education (Draft).* New Delhi: NCTE.

Nachimathu, K. and Vihaya Kumari, G. (1993), An Urgent Need for Environmental Education. *The educational Review,* 4(3), 11-14.

Nuangchalerm, P. and Prachagool, V. (2010), Promoting Transformative Learning of Preservice Teacher through Contemplative Practices. *Asian Social Science,* 6, 95-99.

Pareek, M. and Sidana, A.K. (1998), Environmental Awareness among Secondary School Students. *The Educational Review,* 40(3), 24-30.

Patel, D.G. and Patel, N.A. (1994), Environmental Awareness of the Primary School Teachers. *The Progress of Education,* 18(10), 256-259.

Pradhan, G.C. (1995), Environmental Awareness among Teacher Trainees. *University News,* 33 (40), 10-14.

Pradhan, G.C. (2002), Environmental Awareness among Secondary School Education Teachers. *The Educational Review,* 45(2), 25-27.

Praharaj, B. (1991), *Environmental Knowledge, Environmental Attitude and Perception Regarding Environmental Education Among Pre-service and In-service secondary School Teachers.* Ph.D. Thesis, Maharaja Sayyaji Rao, University of Baroda.

Paneerselvam, *et al.* (1996), *Environmental Science Education.* New Delhi: Sterling Publishers Pvt. Ltd.

Praveen Kumar, Jha (1998), *Manual for Environmental Awareness Ability Measure.* Agra: India National Psychological Corporation.

Prajapat, M.B. (1996), *A Study of the Effect of Programmes Developing Awareness towards Environment among the Pupils in Gandhinagar,* Gujarat. Ph.D. Thesis, Department of Education, Sardar Patel University.

Pushpa Latha, Ahuja (2010), A Study of Environmental Awareness among B.Ed Teacher Trainees of Government aided and Self-financed (Colleges). *Shodh Samiksha aur Mulyankan Research Journal,* 2, 11-12.

Prayoon, Wongchantra and Prasart, Nuangchalerm (2011), Effects of Environmental Ethics Infusion Instruction on Knowledge and Ethics of Undergraduate Students, *Research Journal of Social Science,* 5, 239-243.

Poonam, S. (2010). Environmental Ethics: Theories and Politics. *University News,* 48(24), 14-20.

Palmer, J. (1992). Emergent Understanding of Concepts and Issues in Environmental Science. *International Journal of Science Education,* 24(3), 26-30.

Peal, D.G. (1995), An Investigation into the Environmental Awareness and Enhancement in the Secondary Schools. *Journal of Moral Education,* 26(4), 473-489.

Patel Nanubhai, D. (1995), An Investigation in to the Environmental Awareness of Science Students and Effect of Environmental Studies. *Progress in Education*, 72(2), 26-29.

Ram, S. (2006), *Current Issues in Teacher Education*. New Delhi: Sarup and Sons.

Rao Digumarti Bhaskara (1996), *Encyclopaedia of Education for All*. (5 Volumes). New Delhi: APH Publishing Corporation.

Rajput, J.S. and Gupta, V.P. (1988), Environmental Awareness among Children of Non-formal Education Centres of M.P. and Maharastra. *Indian Education Review*, 119-125.

Raju, G. (2007), Environmental Ethics of Higher Secondary Students. *Edutracks*, 6(11), 32-35.

Reddy, K.P. and Reddy, D.N. (2002), *Environmental Education*. Hyderabad: Neelkamal Publications Pvt. Ltd.

Rakesh, Chandra (1980), Environmental Pollution in Urban Areas. *Indian Architect*, 22(100), 56-69.

Rao, K. (2010), Environmental Awareness among D.Ed. Students. *International Referred Research Journal*, 2(18), 16-18.

Santosh Kumar, Rout and Sukriti, Agarwal (2006), Environmental Awareness and Environmental Attitude of Students at High School Level. *Edutracks*, 6(1), 25-26.

Sarla, Rajput (2004). Environmental Study, *Encyclopaedia of Indian Education*, 1, 659-663.

Sargunam Davidson, S. (2010), Participatory Programmes in Environmental Education Awareness at the Primary and Middle Levels. *Edutracks*, 10(4), 23-24.

Saraswathi, Ratkalla (2006), Environmental Protection Act. *A Weekly Journal of Higher Education*, 44(12), 85-90.

Singh, R.P. and Sharma, Sandhir (2004), *Teaching of Environment: New Trends and Innovations*. New Delhi: Deep and Deep Publications.

Singh, Y.K. (2005), *Teaching of Environmental Science*. New Delhi: APH Publishing Corporation.

Singh, Y.K. (2005), *Teaching of Zoology*. New Delhi: APH Publishing Corporation.

Singh, N. (1999), Environmental Education: A Forgotten Commitment. *University News*, 37, 14-16.

Sharma, R.A. (2001), *Environmental Education*. Meerut: Surya Publications.

Sharma, P.D. (1994), *Ecology and Environment*. Meerut: Rastogi Publications.

Sharma, A. (1997), Developing a Global Environmental Perspective in the School Curriculum in India. *International Journal of Environmental Education and Information*, 16(3), 237-250.

Samir, K. (2005), Awareness of Environmental Education among the Post Graduate Students. *Edutracks*, 4(12), 35-38.

Smriti, Bhosle (2006), Environmental Education in Schools. *A weekly Journal of Higher Education*, 44(12), 110-114.

Seeni, S. and Manickam, V.S. (2002), Environmental Education for the Masses: The Darwin Approach. *Research and Reflection on Education*, 1(2), 23-28.

Sebastian, S. and Nima, D. (2005), Awareness of Biodiversity and Its Conservation among Higher Secondary School Students in Negyatinkara Education District. *Research and Reflection on Education*, 3(2), 3-8.

Shikhadhar, K. (2007), Environmental Awareness among College Level Students. *Journal of Education Studies*, 5(1), 19-12.

Shaila, V. (2003), *Effect of Background Variables on the Environmental Attitude of Secondary School Teachers*. M.Ed. Dissertation. Department of Education, Bangalore University.

Sahaya Mary, R. and Paul Raj, I. (2005), Environmental Awareness among High School Students. *Edutracks*, 5(4), 33-35.

Sandhya, Gihar (2006), Environmental Responsibility among Students. *Edutracks*, 6(1), 23-27.

Selvam, M., Anto Boopalarayan, G. and William Dharma Raja, B. (2003), Environmental Awareness among the Rural and Urban Trainees. *Research and Reflections on Education*, 1 (1), 40-46.

Shiva Kumar, K. and Mangala Patil, S. (2007), Influence of Environmental Educational on Environmental Attitude of the Post-graduate Students. *Edutracks*, 6(8), 34-36.

Sadhana, T. (2007), *Our NGS Green Life*. Hyderabad: Andhra Pradesh National Green Corps.

Sabhlok, R. (1995), A Study of the Awareness and Attitude of the Teachers and Students of High Schools towards Environmental Education in Jabalpur District. *Indian Education Abstract*, 1(24), 62-63.

Shahnawaj, N. (1990), *Environmental Awareness and Environmental Attitude of Secondary and Higher Secondary School Teachers and Students*. Ph.D. Education, Rajasthan University.

Shabina Jinarajan, A.K. (1999), *A Study of Environmental Awareness and Attitude Towards Environmental Education of Student Teacher of Banglore City*. M.Phil Dissertation, Department of Education, Bangalore University.

Shaila, V. (2003), *Effect of Background Variables on the Environmental Attitude of Secondary School Teachers*. M.Ed. Dissertation, Department of Education, Bangalore University.

Shobeiri, S.M. (2005), *A Comparative Study of Environmental Awareness and Attitude of Teachers and Students of Secondary Schools in India and Iran*. Ph.D. Thesis, Department of Education, University of Mysore.

Sharma, P.D. (1994), *Ecology and Environment*. Meerut: Rastogi Publications.

Singh, K. (1996), *Education for the Global Society – Learning the Treasure Within*. France: UNESCO.

Shanawaj, N. (1990), *Environmental Awareness and Environmental Attitude of Secondary and Higher Secondary School Teachers and Students*. Ph.D. Education, Rajasthan University.

Saheblal Mahiboob, Nadaf (2011), A Study of Environmental Awareness of B.Ed. Teacher Trainees in Relation to Their Personality Factors, Self-concept and Study Habits. *International Referred Research Journal*, 3, 159-164.

Spady, W. (1977), Competency-based Education: A Bandwagon in Search of a Definition. *Educational Research*, 6, 9-14.

Stapp, W., Caduto, M., Mann, L. and Nowak, P. (1980), Analysis of Pre-service Environmental Education of Teachers in Europe and an Instructional Model for Furthering this Education. *Journal of Environmental Education*, 12(2), 3-10.

Shobeiri, S.M. and Prahallada, N.N. (2006), Environmental Awareness Among Secondary School Students in India and Iran. *Edutracks*, 5(6), 27-33.

Sarojini, K. (2010), Level of Environmental Awareness among the School Students. *Edutracks*, 9(10), 41-43.

Tripathi, M.P. (2000), A Comparative Study of Environmental Awareness of Students Studying in Central Schools and Other Schools at 10+Level in Uttar Pradesh. *National Journal of Education*, 6(1), 47-51.

United Nations (2007), Report on Scientific Findings for Policy-makers. *Deccan Herald*, 2(34), 1-4.

UGC (2003), *Six Months Module Syllabus for Environmental Studies for Under Graduate Courses*. New Delhi: UGC.

UNESCO-EPD (1997), *Environment and Society: Education and Public Awareness for Sustainability*. Paper Prepared for UNESCO International Conference, Thessalonki.

UNESCO (1985), *Environmental Education Module for Pre-sevice Training of Social Science Teachers and Supervisors of Secondary Schools*. UNESCO-UNEP.

UNESCO (1985), *Environmental Education Module for In-sevice Training of Social Science Teachers and Supervisors of Secondary Schools*. UNESCO-UNEP.

UNESCO (1986), *Environmental Education Module for In-sevice Training of Social Science Teachers and Supervisors of Secondary Schools:* Division of Science and Technology and Vocational Education. UNESCO-UNEP.

UNESCO (1988), *Environmental Education Approach to the Training of Elementary Teachers: A Teacher Training Programme*. UNESCO-UNEP.

Vlaardingerbroek, Barend and Taylor, T.G. (2007), The Environmental Knowledge and Attitudes of Prospective Teachers in Lebanon. *International Research in Geographical and Environmental Education*, 6(2), 120-134.

Vipinder, S. and Jaswinder, S.D. (2005), Environmental Educational Awareness among Elementary School Teachers. *Perspective in Education*, 21(2), 117-122.

Yeshodhara, K. and Asha, B.N. (2005), *Role of NGO's in Promoting Non-formal Environmental Education – A Case Study in Bangalore District*. SRTT Project Report Submitted to Institute for Social and Economic Change, Nagarabhavi, Bangalore.

Yeshodhara, K. and Larijani, Maryam (2008), An Empirical Study of Environmental Attitude among Higher Primary School Teachers of India and Iran. *Journal of Human Ecology*, 24(3), 195-200.

Additional Reading

Bhaskara Rao, Digumarti (1994), *Scientific Aptitude*. New Delhi: Ashish Publishing House. ISBN 81-7024-658-X.

Bhaskara Rao, Digumarti (1995), *Animal Kingdom*. New Delhi: Discovery Publishing House. ISBN 81-7141-274-2.

Bhaskara Rao, Digumarti (1995), *Batracology*. New Delhi: Discovery Publishing House. ISBN 81-7141-279-3.

Bhaskara Rao, Digumarti (1997), *Scientific Attitude*. New Delhi: Discovery Publishing House. ISBN 81-7141-381-1.

Bhaskara Rao, Digumarti (1996), *Scientific Attitude vis-à-vis Scientific Aptitude*. New Delhi: Discovery Publishing House. ISBN 81-7141-308-0.

Bhaskara Rao, Digumarti (2004), *Scientific Attitude, Scientific Aptitude and Achievement*. New Delhi: Discovery Publishing House. ISBN 81-7141-781-7.

Bhaskara Rao, Digumarti (2004), *Educational Administration*. New Delhi: Discovery Publishing House. ISBN 81-7141-842-2.

Bhaskara Rao, Digumarti (2004), *Issues in School Education*. New Delhi: Discovery Publishing House. ISBN 81-8356-025-3.

Bhaskara Rao, Digumarti, Editor (1996), *Encyclopaedia of Education* For All, 5 Volumes. New Delhi: APH Publishing Corporation. ISBN 81-7024-759-4 (set).

Vol. I *Education For All: The World Conference*. ISBN 81-7024-760-8.

Vol. II *Education For All: The EPA-9 Summit*. ISBN 81-7024-761-6.

Vol. III *Education For All: Quality Education For All*. ISBN 81-7024-762-6.

Vol. IV *Education For All: Planning and Monitoring*. ISBN 81-7024-763-4.

Vol. V *Education For All: The Indian Scenario*. ISBN 81-7024-764-0.

Bhaskara Rao, Digumarti, Editor (1999), *International Encyclopaedia of AIDS*, 11 Volumes. New Delhi: Discovery Publishing House. ISBN 81-7141-522-6 (set).

Vol. 1. *Introduction to HIV/AIDS*. ISBN 81-7141-523-7.

Vol. 2. *HIV/AIDS – Issues and Challenges*, 2 Parts. ISBN 81-7141-524-5.

Vol. 3. *HIV/AIDS – Socio-economic Realities*. ISBN 81-7141-524-3.

Vol. 4. *HIV/AIDS – Law Ethics and Human Rights*, 2 Parts. ISBN 81-7141-526-1.

Vol. 5. *AIDS and NGOs*. ISBN 81-7141-527-X.

Vol. 6. *AIDS and Home Care*. ISBN 81-7141-528-8.

Vol. 7. *STD Case Management*. ISBN 81-7141-529-6.

Vol. 8. *HIV/AIDS Prevention and Care – Teaching Modules for Nurses and Midwives*. ISBN 81-7141-530-X.

Vol. 9. *HIV Prevention Education for Educational Institutions*. ISBN 81-7141-531-8.

Vol.10. *Instructional Modules for AIDS Education*. ISBN 81-7141-532-6.

Vol.11. *School Health Education to Prevent AIDS and STD – A Package for Curriculum Planners*. ISBN 81-7141-533-4.

Bhaskara Rao, Digumarti, Editor (2000), *International Encyclopaedia of Human Rights*, 7 Volumes in 13 Parts. New Delhi: Discovery Publishing House. ISBN 81-7141-567-9 (set).

Vol. 1. *International Instruments of Human Rights*, 2 Parts. ISBN 81-7141-569-4.

Vol. 2. *Regional Instruments of Human Rights*. ISBN 81-7141-604-7.

Vol. 3. *Human Rights and the United Nations,* 2 Parts. ISBN 81-7141-605-5.

Vol. 4. *Fact Files of Human Rights,* 3 Parts. ISBN 81-7141-606-3.

Vol. 5. *Study Stories of Human Rights,* 3 Parts. ISBN 81-7141-607-3.

Vol. 6. *International Meetings on Human Rights,* 2 Parts. ISBN 81-714-608-X.

Vol. 7. *Professional Training in Human Rights.* ISBN 81-7141-609-8.

Bhaskara Rao, Digumarti, Editor (2000), *International Encyclopaedia of Science and Technology Education,* 11 Volumes. New Delhi: Discovery Publishing House. ISBN 81-7141-548-2 (set).

Vol. 1. *Science and Technology Education.* ISBN 81-7141-568-7.

Vol. 2. *Science Education in Developing Countries.* ISBN 81-7141-569-9.

Vol. 3. *Organizational Structure of Science.* ISBN 81-7141-570-9.

Vol. 4. *Science Education in Asia and the Pacific.* ISBN 81-7141-571-7

Vol. 5. *Science and Technology Education For All.* ISBN 81-7141-572-5.

Vol. 6. *Values, Ethics, Talent and Girls in Science and Technology Education.* ISBN 81-7141-573-3.

Vol. 7. *Popularization of Science and Technology Education.* ISBN 81-7141-574-1.

Vol. 8. *Science, Power and Society.* ISBN 81-7141- 575-X.

Vol. 9. *Information Technology.* ISBN 81-7141-576-8.

Vol.10. *Teacher Training in Science and Technology Education.* ISBN 81-7142-577-6.

Vol.11. *Teacher Training in Science and Technology: A Curriculum Framework.* ISBN 81-7141-578-4.

Bhaskara Rao, Digumarti, Editor (2000), *Education For All: Achieving the Goal,* 3 Volumes. New Delhi: APH Publishing Corporation. ISBN 81-7648-152-1 (set).

Vol. I *The Global Consensus.* ISBN 81-7648-155-6.

Vol. II *Mid-Decade Review Reports of Regional Seminars.* ISBN 81-7648-154-8.

Vol. III *Issues and Trends.* ISBN 81-7648-155-6.

Bhaskara Rao, Digumarti, Editor (2004), *International Encyclopaedia of Learning to Live Together*, 4 Volumes. New Delhi: Discovery Publishing House. ISBN 81-7141-848-1.

Vol. 1. *International Conference on Learning to Live Together.*

Vol. 2. *Globalization and Living Together.*

Vol. 3. *Curriculum for Learning to Live Together.*

Vol. 4. *Science Education for the Contemporary Society.*

Bhaskara Rao, Digumarti, Editor (2005), *Encyclopaedia of Education For All*, 3 Volumes. New Delhi: Discovery Publishing House. ISBN 81-7141-647-0 (set).

Bhaskara Rao, Digumarti, Editor (2007), *Encyclopaedia of Teacher Education*, 4 Volumes. New Delhi: Discovery Publishing House. ISBN 81-8356-306-6 (set).

Bhaskara Rao, Digumarti, Editor (2007), *Encyclopaedia of Education for Living Together*, 4 Volumes. New Delhi: Discovery Publishing House. ISBN 81-7141-848-1 (set).

Bhaskara Rao, Digumarti, Editor (1996), *National Policy on Education*, 2 Volumes. New Delhi: Anmol Publications Pvt. Ltd. ISBN 81-7488-323-1.

Bhaskara Rao, Digumarti, Editor (1996), *Global Perceptions on Peace Education*, 3 Volumes. New Delhi: Discovery Publishing House. ISBN 81-7141-319-6.

Bhaskara Rao, Digumarti, Editor (1997), *Education for the 21st Century.* New Delhi: Discovery Publishing House. ISBN 81-7141-389-7.

Bhaskara Rao, Digumarti, Editor (1997), *Reflections on Scientific Attitude.* New Delhi: Discovery Publishing House. ISBN 81-7141-319-6.

Bhaskara Rao, Digumarti, Editor (1997), *Success Story of A Primary Education Project.* New Delhi: APH Publishing Corporation. ISBN 81-7024-850-7.

Bhaskara Rao, Digumarti, Editor (1997), *World Food Summit.* New Delhi: Discovery Publishing House. ISBN 81-7141-386-2.

Bhaskara Rao, Digumarti, Editor (1997), *Care the Child*, 2 Volumes. New Delhi: Discovery Publishing House. ISBN 81-7141-394-3.

Bhaskara Rao, Digumarti, Editor (1998), *Earth Summit*, 2 Volumes. New Delhi: Discovery Publishing House. ISBN 81-7141-435-4.

Bhaskara Rao, Digumarti, Editor (1998), *Adolescence Education*. New Delhi: Discovery Publishing House. ISBN 81-7141-432-X.

Bhaskara Rao, Digumarti, Editor (1998), *Community and School Nutrition Education*. New Delhi: Discovery Publishing House. ISBN 81-7141-435-4.

Bhaskara Rao, Digumarti, Editor (1998), *District Primary Education Programme*. New Delhi: Discovery Publishing House. ISBN 81-7141-396-X.

Bhaskara Rao, Digumarti, Editor (1998), *National Policy on Education: Towards an Enlightened and Humane Society*. New Delhi: Discovery Publishing House. ISBN 81-7141-426-5.

Bhaskara Rao, Digumarti, Editor (1998), *Reforming School Education*. New Delhi: Discovery Publishing House. ISBN 81-7141-403-6.

Bhaskara Rao, Digumarti, Editor (1998), *Teacher Education in India*. New Delhi: Discovery Publishing House. ISBN 81-7141-406-0.

Bhaskara Rao, Digumarti, Editor (1998), *World Summit for Social Development*. New Delhi: Discovery Publishing House. ISBN 81-7141-420-6.

Bhaskara Rao, Digumarti, Editor (2001), *Nuclear Materials: Issues and Concerns*, 2 Volumes. New Delhi: Discovery Publishing House. ISBN 81-7141-611-X.

Bhaskara Rao, Digumarti, Editor (2001), *Distance Education in Different Countries*. New Delhi: APH Publishing Corporation. ISBN 81-7648-229-3.

Bhaskara Rao, Digumarti, Editor (2001), *Decentralised Management of Education: Management of Education in Panchayati Raj and Municipal Bodies*. New Delhi: Discovery Publishing House. ISBN 81-7141-617-9.

Bhaskara Rao, Digumarti, Editor (2001), *Electrochemistry for Environmental Protection.* New Delhi: Discovery Publishing House. ISBN 81-7141-619-5.

Bhaskara Rao, Digumarti, Editor (2001), *Global Educational Studies.* New Delhi: Discovery Publishing House. ISBN 81-7141-616-0.

Bhaskara Rao, Digumarti, Editor (2001), *Global Synthesis of Educational Assessment.* New Delhi: Discovery Publishing House. ISBN 81-7141-613-6.

Bhaskara Rao, Digumarti, Editor (2001), *Jomtein Decade of Education.* New Delhi: Discovery Publishing House. ISBN 81-7141-618-7.

Bhaskara Rao, Digumarti, Editor (2001), *World Conference on Education for All.* New Delhi: APH Publishing Corporation. ISBN 81-7141-274-9.

Bhaskara Rao, Digumarti, Editor (2001), *World Conference on Higher Education.* New Delhi: Discovery Publishing House. ISBN 81-7141-610-1.

Bhaskara Rao, Digumarti, Editor (2001), *World Conference on Science.* New Delhi: Discovery Publishing House. ISBN 81-7141-612-8.

Bhaskara Rao, Digumarti, Editor (2003), *Inspiring Experiences in Teacher Education.* New Delhi: Discovery Publishing House. ISBN 81-7141-656-X.

Bhaskara Rao, Digumarti, Editor (2003), *International Studies in Education,* 3 Volumes. New Delhi: Discovery Publishing House. ISBN 81-7141-647-0.

Bhaskara Rao, Digumarti, Editor (2003), *Military Conversion: Impact on Science and Technology.* New Delhi: Discovery Publishing House. ISBN 81-7141-578-4.

Bhaskara Rao, Digumarti, Editor (2003), *United Nations Millennium Summit.* New Delhi: Discovery Publishing House. ISBN 81-7141-632-2.

Bhaskara Rao, Digumarti, Editor (2003), *World Assembly on Aging.* New Delhi: Discovery Publishing House. ISBN 81-7141-637-3.

Bhaskara Rao, Digumarti, Editor (2003), *World Conference on Human Rights*. New Delhi: Discovery Publishing House. ISBN 81-7141-661-6.

Bhaskara Rao, Digumarti, Editor (2003), *World Education Forum*. New Delhi: Discovery Publishing House. ISBN 81-7141-639-X.

Bhaskara Rao, Digumarti, Editor (2003), *Education, Employment and Human Resource Development*. New Delhi: Discovery Publishing House. ISBN 81-7141-681-0.

Bhaskara Rao, Digumarti, Editor (2003), *Successful Schooling*. New Delhi: Discovery Publishing House. ISBN 81-7141-677-2.

Bhaskara Rao, Digumarti, Editor (2003), *European Education and Teachers*. New Delhi: Discovery Publishing House. ISBN 81-7141-702-7.

Bhaskara Rao, Digumarti, Editor (2003), *Teachers in a Changing World*. New Delhi: Discovery Publishing House. ISBN 81-7141-694-2.

Bhaskara Rao, Digumarti, Editor (2004), *International Guidelines on Open and Distance Teacher Education*. New Delhi: Discovery Publishing House. ISBN 81-7141-777-9.

Bhaskara Rao, Digumarti, Editor (2004), *Adult Learning in the 21st Century*. New Delhi: Discovery Publishing House. ISBN 81-7141-797-3.

Bhaskara Rao, Digumarti, Editor (2004), *Educational Practices: Research and Recommendations*. New Delhi: Discovery Publishing House. ISBN 81-7141-835-X.

Bhaskara Rao, Digumarti, Editor (2004), *General Secondary Education in the 21st Century*. New Delhi: Discovery Publishing House. ISBN 81-7141-885-6.

Bhaskara Rao, Digumarti, Editor (2004), *Reforming Secondary Education*. New Delhi: Discovery Publishing House. ISBN 81-7141-843-0.

Bhaskara Rao, Digumarti, Editor (2004), *Human Rights Education*. New Delhi: Discovery Publishing House. ISBN 81-7141-882-1.

Bhaskara Rao, Digumarti, Editor (2004), *United Nations Decade for Human Rights Education*. New Delhi: Discovery Publishing House. ISBN 81-7141-887-2.

Bhaskara Rao, Digumarti, Editor (2004), *Technical and Vocational Education and Training in the 21st Century*. New Delhi: Discovery Publishing House. ISBN 81-7141-984-4.

Bhaskara Rao, Digumarti, Editor (2005), *Encyclopaedia of Education For All*, 3 Volumes. New Delhi: Discovery Publishing House. ISBN 978-81-8356-905 7.

Bhaskara Rao, Digumarti, Editor (2011), *Right to Education*. Hyderabad: Neel Kamal Publishers. ISBN 81-7648-470-9, 978-81-8316-284-5.

Bhaskara Rao, Digumarti, Editor (2011), *International Encyclopaedia of Educational Policies*. Hyderabad: Neel Kamal Publishers.

Bhaskara Rao, Digumarti, Editor (2012), *Inclusive Education and Policy Frameworks*. New Delhi: Discovery Publishing House. ISBN 978-93-5056-273-4

Bhaskara Rao, Digumarti, Editor (2011), *International Encyclopaedia of Educational Practices*. Hyderabad: Neel Kamal Publications. ISBN 978-81-8316-337-8.

Bhaskara Rao, Digumarti, Editor (2013), *International Encyclopaedia of Education*. Hyderabad: Neel Kamal Publications. ISBN 978-81-8316-350-7.

Bhaskara Rao, Digumarti, Editor (2013), *International Encyclopaedia of Psychology*. Hyderabad: Neel Kamal Publications.

Bhaskara Rao, Digumarti, Editor (2013), *International Encyclopaedia of Psychologists*. Hyderabad: Neel Kamal Publications.

Bhaskara Rao, Digumarti, Editor (2013), *International Encyclopaedia of Philosophy*. Hyderabad: Neel Kamal Publications.

Bhaskara Rao, Digumarti, Editor (2013), *International Encyclopaedia of Philosophers*. Hyderabad: Neel Kamal Publications.

Bhaskara Rao, Digumarti, Editor (2013), *International Encyclopaedia of Linguistcs*. Hyderabad: Neel Kamal Publications.

Bhaskara Rao, Digumarti, Editor (2013), *International Encyclopaedia of Sociology*. Hyderabad: Neel Kamal Publications.

Bhaskara Rao, Digumarti, Editor (2013), *International Encyclopaedia of Sociologists*. Hyderabad: Neel Kamal Publications.

Bhaskara Rao, Digumarti and Marlow Ediger (2013), *Communicative English*. New Delhi: Discovery Publishing House. ISBN 978-93-5056-465-3.

Bhaskara Rao, Digumarti and Marlow Ediger (2013), *Methods of Teaching English*. New Delhi: Discovery Publishing House. ISBN 81-7141-809-0.

Bhaskara Rao, Digumarti and B.S.V. Dutt, Editors (2003), *Education: Programmes and Policies*. New Delhi: APH Publishing Corporation. ISBN 81-7648-470-9.

Bhaskara Rao, Digumarti, C.A.P. Swamy and B.S.V. Dutt (1997), *Self-evaluation in Student Teaching*. New Delhi: Discovery Publishing House. ISBN 81-7141-374-9.

Bhaskara Rao, Digumarti and C. D. Swarna Lattha, Editors (2006), *Encyclopaedia of Biotechnology*, 5 Volumes. New Delhi: Discovery Publishing House. ISBN 81-8356-168-3 (set).

Bhaskara Rao, Digumarti, C. Sridevi and K. Vijaya (1995), *Achievement in Social Studies*. New Delhi: Discovery Publishing House. ISBN 81-7141-281-5.

Bhaskara Rao, Digumarti and D. Naresh Kumar (2004), *School Teacher Effectiveness*. New Delhi: Discovery Publishing House. ISBN 81-7141-782-5.

Bhaskara Rao, Digumarti and D. Sridhar (2002), *Job Satisfaction of School Teachers*. New Delhi: Discovery Publishing House. ISBN 81-7141-652-7.

Bhaskara Rao, Digumarti and Digumarti Pushpa Latha, Editors (1998), *International Encyclopaedia of Women*, 5 Volumes. New Delhi: Discovery Publishing House. ISBN 81-7141-410-9 (set).

Vol. 1. *Status of World's Women*. ISBN 81-7141- 494-X.

Vol. 2. *Women, Education and Empowerment*. ISBN 81-7141-498-1.

Vol. 3. *Women Challenges and Advancement*. ISBN 81-7141-497-4.

Vol. 4. *Women and Family Health*. ISBN 81-7141- 497-4.

Vol. 5. *Women and International Action*. ISBN 81-7141-498-2.

Bhaskara Rao, Digumarti and Digumarti Pushpa Latha (1994), *Achievement in Biology*. New Delhi: Discovery Publishing House. ISBN 81-7141-264-5.

Bhaskara Rao, Digumarti and Digumarti Pushpa Latha (1995), *Achievement in English*. New Delhi: Discovery Publishing House. ISBN 81-7141-283-1.

Bhaskara Rao, Digumarti and Digumarti Pushpa Latha (1994), *Achievement in Science*. New Delhi: Discovery Publishing House. ISBN 81-7141-280-70.

Bhaskara Rao, Digumarti and Digumarti Pushpa Latha (1995), *Achievement in Mathematics*. New Delhi: Discovery Publishing House. ISBN 81-7141-278-5.

Bhaskara Rao, Digumarti and Digumarti Pushpa Latha (2004), *Education for Women*. New Delhi: Discovery Publishing House. ISBN 81-7141-873-2.

Bhaskara Rao, Digumarti, Digumarti Pushpa Latha and Digumarthi Harshitha, Editors (2001), *Biological Warfare*. New Delhi: Discovery Publishing House. ISBN 81-7141-597-0.

Bhaskara Rao, Digumarti, Digumarti Pushpa Latha and Digumarthi Harshitha, Editors (2001), *Women as Educators*. New Delhi: Discovery Publishing House. ISBN 81-7141-602-0.

Bhaskara Rao, Digumarti and Digumarthi Harshitha (2004), *Adjustment of Adolescents*. New Delhi: APH Publishing House. ISBN 81-7648-836-8.

Bhaskara Rao, Digumarti and Digumarthi Harshitha, Editors (2001), *Education in India*. New Delhi: APH Publishing House. ISBN 81-7648-207-2.

Bhaskara Rao, Digumarti, Digumarti Pushpa Latha and Digumarthi Harshitha, Editors (2001). *Assessing Learning Achievement*. New Delhi: Discovery Publishing House. ISBN 81-7141-601-2.

Bhaskara Rao, Digumarti, Digumarti Pushpa Latha and Digumarthi Harshitha, Editors (2001), *Energy Security*. New Delhi: Discovery Publishing House. ISBN 81-7141-598-9.

Bhaskara Rao, Digumarti, Digumarthi Harshitha and K.R.S. Sambasiva Rao, Editors (1999), *Advanced Biotechnology*. New Delhi: Discovery Publishing House. ISBN 81-7141-516-4.

Bhaskara Rao, Digumarti and K.R.S. Sambasiva Rao, Editors (1996), *Current Trends in Indian Education*. New Delhi: Discovery Publishing House. ISBN 81-7141-311-0.

Bhaskara Rao, Digumarti and D. Naresh Kumar (2004), *School Teacher Effectiveness*. New Delhi: Discovery Publishing House. ISBN 81-7141-782-5.

Bhaskara Rao, Digumarti and E. Sreekanth Babu (2004), *Educational Interests of School Students*. New Delhi: Discovery Publishing House. ISBN 81-7141-837-6.

Bhaskara Rao, Digumarti and K. Vijaya (1995), *A Text Book Evaluation*. Ambala Cantt: The Associated Publishers.

Bhaskara Rao, Digumarti and M.A. Fayaz (2004), *Problems of Primary School Drop-outs*. New Delhi: Discovery Publishing House. ISBN 81-7141- 834-1.

Bhaskara Rao, Digumarti and N.V.M. Mohana Rao (2002), *Problems of Mentally Handicapped Children*. New Delhi: Discovery Publishing House. ISBN 81-7141- 645-4.

Bhaskara Rao, Digumarti and S. Chandra Mohan (2002), *Sports Management*. New Delhi: APH Publishing House. ISBN 81-7648-467-9.

Bhaskara Rao, Digumarti and S.A. Khader (2004), *Problems of Private School Teachers*. New Delhi: Discovery Publishing Corporation. ISBN 81-7141-838-4.

Bhaskara Rao, Digumarti and S.A. Khader (2004), *School Education in India*. New Delhi: Discovery Publishing Corporation. ISBN 81-7141-849-X.

Bhaskara Rao, Digumarti and SK. Johni Basha (2004), *Teachers' Population Education Awareness*. New Delhi: Discovery Publishing House. ISBN 81-7141-832-5.

Bhaskara Rao, Digumarti, V.V. Rao, V.V. Lakshmi and V.V. Krishna, Editors (1999), *Status and Advancement of Women*. New Delhi: APH Publishing Corporation. ISBN 81-7648-169-6.

Babu, P.C., Author and Digumarti Bhaskara Rao, Editor (2004), *Flowers of Wisdom*. New Delhi: Discovery Publishing House. ISBN 81-7141-695-0.

Babu, P.C., Author and Digumarti Bhaskara Rao, Editor (2008), *Worlds of Wisdom*. New Delhi: Discovery Publishing House.

Bujji Babu, K., author and Digumarti Bhaskara Rao, Editor (2007), *Teaching Aptitude of Primary School Teachers*. New Delhi: Sonali Publications. ISBN 81-8411-083-9.

Amala, P. A. and Anupama, P., Authors and Digumarti Bhaskara Rao, Editor (2004), *History of Education*. New Delhi: Discovery Publishing House. ISBN 81-7141-860-0.

Bhagya Lakshmi, L., Author and Digumarti Bhaskara Rao, Editor (2000), *Reading and Comprehension*. New Delhi: Discovery Publishing House. ISBN 81-7141-543-1.

Bhasha, S.A., Author and Digumarti Bhaskara Rao, Editor (2004), *Methods of Teaching Geography*. New Delhi: Discovery Publishing House. ISBN 81-7141-807-4.

Bhuvaneswara Lakshmi, Gadde, Author and Digumarti Bhaskara Rao, Editor (2000), *Attitude Towards Science*. New Delhi: Discovery Publishing House. ISBN 81-7141-541-6.

Bhuvaneswara Lakshmi, G., Author and Digumarti Bhaskara Rao, Editor (2004), *Methods of Teaching Life Science*. New Delhi: Discovery Publishing House. ISBN 81-7141-804-X.

Bhuvaneswara Lakshmi, G. and K. Subba Rao, Authors and Digumarti Bhaskara Rao, Editor (2004), *Methods of Teaching Biology*. New Delhi: Discovery Publishing House. ISBN 81-7141-914-3.

Chary, K.V.N.B., Author and Digumarti Bhaskara Rao, Editor (2006), *Techniques of Teaching Physics*. New Delhi: Sonali Publications. ISBN 81-8411-046-4.

Chowdary, S.B.J.R. and Naga Raju, Authors and Digumarti Bhaskara Rao, Editor (2004), *Mastery of Teaching Skills.* New Delhi: Discovery Publishing House. ISBN 81-7141-861-9.

Dayakara Reddy, V. and Digumarti Bhaskara Rao, Editors (2006), *Value-Oriented Education.* New Delhi: Discovery Publishing House. ISBN 81-8356-051-2

Devraj, T.A.S., Author and Digumarti Bhaskara Rao, Editor (1997), *Trace Analysis of Uranium and Thorium.* New Delhi: Discovery Publishing House. ISBN 81-7141-375-7.

Durga Rani, K., Author and Digumarti Bhaskara Rao, Editor (2000), *Educational Aspirations and Scientific Attitudes.* New Delhi: Discovery Publishing House. ISBN 81-7141-555-5.

Durga Prasad, V., Author and Digumarti Bhaskara Rao, Editor (2012), *Problems of Tribal Girl Students.* New Delhi: Discovery Publishing House. ISBN 978-93-5056-399-1.

Dutt, B.S.V. and Digumarti Bhaskara Rao (2001), *Empowering Primary Teachers.* New Delhi: Discovery Publishing House. ISBN 81-7141-615-2.

Dutt, B.S.V., Author and Digumarti Bhaskara Rao, Editor (2004), *Comparative Education.* New Delhi: Discovery Publishing House. ISBN 81-7141-912-7.

Ediger, Marlow and Digumarti Bhaskara Rao, Editors (2006), *Encyclopaedia of School Education,* 5 Volumes. New Delhi: Discovery Publishing House. ISBN 81-8356-308-2 (set).

Ediger, Marlow and Digumarti Bhaskara Rao, Editors (2006), *Encyclopaedia of School Administration,* 4 Volumes. New Delhi: Discovery Publishing House. ISBN 81-8356-307-4 (set).

Ediger, Marlow and Digumarti Bhaskara Rao, Editors (2007), *Encyclopaedia of School Curriculum,* 10 Volumes. New Delhi: Discovery Publishing House. ISBN 81-8356-305-8 (set).

Ediger, Marlow and Digumarti Bhaskara Rao, Editors (2007), *Encyclopaedia of Teaching,* 8 Volumes. New Delhi: Discovery Publishing House. ISBN 81-8356-305-8 (set).

Marlow Ediger and Digumarti Bhaskara Rao, Editors (2006), *Encyclopaedia of School Education*, 5 Volumes. New Delhi: Discovery Publishing House. ISBN 81-8356-308-2 (set).

Marlow Ediger and Digumarti Bhaskara Rao, Editors (2006), *Encyclopaedia of School Administration*, 4 Volumes. New Delhi: Discovery Publishing House. ISBN 81-8356-307-4 (set).

Marlow Ediger and Digumarti Bhaskara Rao, Editors (2007), *Encyclopaedia of School Curriculum*, 10 Volumes. New Delhi: Discovery Publishing House. ISBN 81-8356-305-8 (set).

Marlow Ediger and Digumarti Bhaskara Rao, Editors (2007), *Encyclopaedia of Teaching*, 8 Volumes. New Delhi: Discovery Publishing House. ISBN 81-8356-305-8 (set).

Ediger, Marlow and Digumarti Bhaskara Rao (1996), *Science Curriculum*. New Delhi: Discovery Publishing House. ISBN 81-7141-321-8.

Ediger, Marlow and Digumarti Bhaskara Rao (2000), *Teaching Mathematics Successfully*. New Delhi: Discovery Publishing House. ISBN 81-7141-552-0.

Ediger, Marlow and Digumarti Bhaskara Rao (2001), *Teaching Science Successfully*. New Delhi: Discovery Publishing House. ISBN 81-7141-600-4.

Ediger, Marlow and Digumarti Bhaskara Rao (2001), *Teaching Social Studies Successfully*. New Delhi: Discovery Publishing House. ISBN 81-7141-596-2.

Ediger, Marlow and Digumarti Bhaskara Rao (2002), *Philosophy and Curriculum*. New Delhi: Discovery Publishing House. ISBN 81-7141-631-4.

Ediger, Marlow and Digumarti Bhaskara Rao (2002), *Improving School Administration*. New Delhi: Discovery Publishing House. ISBN 81-7141-633-0.

Ediger, Marlow and Digumarti Bhaskara Rao (2002), *Elementary Curriculum*. New Delhi: Discovery Publishing House. ISBN 81-7141-658-6.

Ediger, Marlow and Digumarti Bhaskara Rao (2003), *Language Arts Curriculum*. New Delhi: Discovery Publishing House. ISBN 81-7141-657-8.

Ediger, Marlow and Digumarti Bhaskara Rao (2003), *Psychology and Curriculum.* New Delhi: Discovery Publishing House. ISBN 81-7141-691-8.

Ediger, Marlow and Digumarti Bhaskara Rao (2003), *Teaching Language Arts Successfully.* New Delhi: Discovery Publishing House. ISBN 81-7141-678-0.

Ediger, Marlow and Digumarti Bhaskara Rao (2003), *School Curriculum and Administration.* New Delhi: Discovery Publishing House. ISBN 81-7141-709-4.

Ediger, Marlow and Digumarti Bhaskara Rao (2003), *Teaching Mathematics in Elementary Schools.* New Delhi: Discovery Publishing House. ISBN 81-7141-687-X.

Ediger, Marlow and Digumarti Bhaskara Rao (2003), *Teaching Science in Elementary Schools.* New Delhi: Discovery Publishing House. ISBN 81-7141-698-5.

Ediger, Marlow and Digumarti Bhaskara Rao (2003), *School Curriculum and Administration.* New Delhi: Discovery Publishing House. ISBN 81-7141-709-4.

Ediger, Marlow and Digumarti Bhaskara Rao (2003), *Elementary Curriculum Improvement.* New Delhi: Discovery Publishing House. ISBN 81-7141-740-X.

Ediger, Marlow and Digumarti Bhaskara Rao (2004), *School Organisation.* New Delhi: Discovery Publishing House. ISBN 81-7141-843-0.

Ediger, Marlow and Digumarti Bhaskara Rao (2004), *Relevancy in Elementary Curriculum.* New Delhi: Discovery Publishing House. ISBN 81-7141-845-9.

Ediger, Marlow and Digumarti Bhaskara Rao (2005), *Quality School Education.* New Delhi: Discovery Publishing House. ISBN 81-8356-022-9.

Ediger, Marlow and Digumarti Bhaskara Rao (2006), *Successful School Education.* New Delhi: Discovery Publishing House. ISBN 81-8356-054-7.

Ediger, Marlow and Digumarti Bhaskara Rao (2006), *Successful School Administration.* New Delhi : Discovery Publishing House. ISBN 81-8356-046-6.

Ediger, Marlow and Digumarti Bhaskara Rao (2006), *Issues in School Curruculum.* New Delhi: Discovery Publishing House. ISBN 81-8356-052-0.

Ediger, Marlow and Digumarti Bhaskara Rao (2006), *Community College – Curriculum and Teaching.* New Delhi: Discovery Publishing House. ISBN 81-8356-053-9.

Ediger, Marlow and Digumarti Bhaskara Rao (2006), *Administration of Schools.* New Delhi: Discovery Publishing House. ISBN 81-8356-244-2.

Ediger, Marlow and Digumarti Bhaskara Rao (2006), *Reading Curriculum and Instruction.* New Delhi: Discovery Publishing House. ISBN 81-8356-266-3.

Ediger, Marlow and Digumarti Bhaskara Rao (2006), *Curriculum Organisation.* New Delhi: Discovery Publishing House. ISBN 81-8356-205-1.

Ediger, Marlow and Digumarti Bhaskara Rao (2006), *Curriculum of School Subjects.* New Delhi: Discovery Publishing House. ISBN 81-8356-207-8.

Ediger, Marlow, B.S.V. Dutt and Digumarti Bhaskara Rao (2003), *Teaching English Successfully.* New Delhi: Discovery Publishing House. ISBN 81-7141-707-8.

Ediger, Marlow and Digumarti Bhaskara Rao (2007), *School Science Education.* New Delhi: Discovery Publishing House. ISBN 81-8356-352-X.

Ediger, Marlow and Digumarti Bhaskara Rao (2007), *Language Arts Education.* New Delhi: Discovery Publishing House. ISBN 81-8356-333-3.

Ediger, Marlow and Digumarti Bhaskara Rao (2010), *Effective Schooling.* New Delhi: Discovery Publishing House. ISBN 978-81-8356-613-1.

Ediger, Marlow and Digumarti Bhaskara Rao (2010), *Effective School Curriculum.* New Delhi: Discovery Publishing House. ISBN 978-81-8356-585-1.

Ediger, Marlow and Digumarti Bhaskara Rao (2010), *Essays on Teaching Science.* New Delhi: Discovery Publishing House. ISBN 978-81-8356-882-1.

Ediger, Marlow and Digumarti Bhaskara Rao (2010), *Essays on Teaching Social Studies*. New Delhi: Discovery Publishing House. ISBN 978-81-8356-883-8.

Ediger, Marlow and Digumarti Bhaskara Rao (2010), *Essays on Teaching Reading*. New Delhi: Discovery Publishing House. ISBN 978-81-8356-881-4.

Ediger, Marlow and Digumarti Bhaskara Rao (2011), *Essays on Teaching Mathematics*. New Delhi: Discovery Publishing House. ISBN 978-81-8356-880-7.

Ediger, Marlow and Digumarti Bhaskara Rao (2010), *Essays on Teaching*. New Delhi: Discovery Publishing House.

Ediger, Marlow and Digumarti Bhaskara Rao (2010), *Essays on School Issues*. New Delhi: Discovery Publishing House. ISBN 978-93-5056-264-2.

Elizabeth, M.E.S., Author and Digumarti Bhaskara Rao, Editor (2004), *Methods of Teaching English*. New Delhi: Discovery Publishing House. ISBN 81-7141-809-0.

Elizabeth, M.E.S., Author and Digumarti Bhaskara Rao, Editor (2004), *Acquisition of English Vocabulary*. New Delhi: Discovery Publishing House. ISBN 81-8356-075-X.

Fatima, Sk. Author and Digumarti Bhaskara Rao, Editor (2007), *Reasoning Ability of School Students*. New Delhi: Discovery Publishing House. ISBN 81-8356-330-9.

Fatima, SK. and Digumarti Bhaskara Rao (2008), *Reasoning Ability of Adolescent Students*. New Delhi: Sonali Publications.

Gopala Krishna, M., Author and Digumarti Bhaskara Rao, Editor (2007), *Techniques of Teaching Physical Education*. New Delhi: Sonali Publications. ISBN 81-8411-044-8.

Gopala Krishna, M., Author and Digumarti Bhaskara Rao, Editor (2007), *Techniques of Teaching Education*. New Delhi: Sonali Publications. ISBN 81-8411-062-6.

Harshitha, Digumarthi, Author and Digumarti Bhaskara Rao, Editor (2004), *Methods of Teaching Information Technology*. New Delhi: Discovery Publishing House. ISBN 81-7141-805-8.

Harshitha, Digumarthi, Author and Digumarti Bhaskara Rao, Editor (2007), *Techniques of Teaching Computer Science*. New Delhi: Sonali Publications. ISBN 81-8411-036-7.

Indira Devi, Author and J. Prasanth Kumar and Digumarti Bhaskara Rao, Editors (2004), *Values in Language Text Books*. New Delhi: APH Publishing Corporation.

Jalaja Kumari, C., Author and Digumarti Bhaskara Rao, Editor (2004), *Methods of Teaching Educational Technology*. New Delhi: Discovery Publishing House. ISBN 81-7141-810-4.

Jalaja Kumari, C., Author and Digumarti Bhaskara Rao, Editor (2007), *Job Satisfaction of Teachers*. New Delhi: Discovery Publishing House. ISBN 81-8356-329-5.

Janardhan Reddy, B., Author and Digumarti Bhaskara Rao, Editor (2006), *Techniques of Teaching Sociology*. New Delhi: Sonali Publications. ISBN 81-8411-042-1.

Jayasree, K., Author and Digumarti Bhaskara Rao, Editor (1999), *Correlates of Socialisation*. New Delhi: Discovery Publishing House. ISBN 81-7141-517-2.

Jayasree, K., Author and Digumarti Bhaskara Rao, Editor (2004), *Methods of Teaching Science*. New Delhi: Discovery Publishing House. ISBN 81-7141-801-5.

John Babu, C., Author and T.J.R. Prasad, G.M. Madhukar and Digumarti Bhaskara Rao, Editors (2004). *Problem Solving in Mathematics*. New Delhi: APH Publishing Corporation. ISBN 81-7648-273-0.

Joseph Raju, B and G.A. Anitha, Authors and Digumarti Bhaskara Rao, Editor (2004), *Population Education*. New Delhi: Sonali Publications. ISBN 81-88836-31-3.

Jyosthana, M., Author and Digumarti Bhaskara Rao, Editor (2011), *Achievement Motivation and Achievement in English of School Students*. New Delhi: Discovery Publishing House. ISBN 978-93-5056-002-0.

Lalitha, T., Author and K.S. Prabhakaram, D.S.N. Sastry and Digumarti Bhaskara Rao, Editors (2004), *Educational Philosophic Beliefs*. New Delhi: Discovery Publishing House. ISBN 81-7141-765-5.

Krishna, G., Author and Digumarti Bhaskara Rao, Editor (2006), *Techniques of Teaching Physical Education.* New Delhi: Discovery Publishing House. ISBN 81-8411-044-8.

Kumar Raja, G., Author and Digumarti Bhaskara Rao, Editor (2007), *Principles of Primary School.* New Delhi: Sonali Publications. ISBN 81-8411-054-5.

Lakshmi Kumari, V., Author and Digumarti Bhaskara Rao, Editor (2006), *Techniques of Teaching Home Science.* New Delhi: Discovery Publishing House. ISBN 81-8411-048-0.

Madhava, K., Author and Digumarti Bhaskara Rao, Editor (2008), *Personality of Adolescent Students.* New Delhi: Sonali Publications.

Madhu Bala, Jampala, Author and Digumarti Bhaskara Rao, Editor (2004), *Methods of Teaching Exceptional Children.* New Delhi: Discovery Publishing House. ISBN 81-7141-802-3.

Mallikarjuna Reddy, V., Author and Digumarti Bhaskara Rao, Editor (2011), *Teaching Aptitude, Social Adjustment and Job Satisfaction of Science Teachers.* New Delhi: Discovery Publishing House. ISBN 978-93-5056-121-8.

Marja, Talvi and Digumarti Bhaskara Rao, Editors (1996), *Educational Leadership and Social Changes.* New Delhi: Discovery Publishing House. ISBN 81-7141-320-X.

Naga Kumari, U., Author and Digumarti Bhaskara Rao, Editor (2008), *Science Process Skills of School Students.* New Delhi: Sonali Publications.

Nageswara Rao, S. and M. Srihari, Authors and Digumarti Bhaskara Rao, Editor (2004), *Guidance and Counselling.* New Delhi: Discovery Publishing House. ISBN 81-7141-840-6.

Nageswara Rao, S., Author and Digumarti Bhaskara Rao, Editor (2006), *Techniques of Teaching Psychology.* New Delhi: Discovery Publishing House. ISBN 81-8411-040-5.

Naidu., P. Ch. A., Author and Digumarti Bhaskara Rao, Editor (2007), *Feedback Methods and Student Performance.* New Delhi: Discovery Publishing House. ISBN 81-8356-284-1.

Nageswara Rao, S. and P. Sridhar, Authors and Digumarti Bhaskara Rao, Editor (2004), *Methods and Techniques of Teaching*. New Delhi: Sonali Publications. ISBN 81-88836-33-8.

Nirmala Jyothi, M., Author and Digumarti Bhaskara Rao, Editor (2003), *Non-detention System in School Education.* New Delhi: Discovery Publishing House. ISBN 81-7141-654-3.

Padma Tulasi, G., Author and Digumarti Bhaskara Rao, Editor (2004), *Methods of Teaching Elementary Science.* New Delhi: Discovery Publishing House. ISBN 81-7141-871-6.

Pala Prasada Rao, V., Author and K. N. Rani and D. Bhaskara Rao, Editors (2004), *India Pakistan: Partition Perspectives in Indo English Novels.* New Delhi: Discovery Publishing House. ISBN 81-7141-871-6.

Pala Prasada Rao, V., Author and D. Bhaskara Rao, Editors (2008), *Functioning of Autonomous Colleges.* New Delhi: Sonali Publications.

Pitchi Reddy, M., Author and Digumarti Bhaskara Rao, Editor (2007), *Techniques of Teaching Social Sciences.* New Delhi: Sonali Publications. ISBN 81-8411-066-X.

Prasad Babu, B., Author and P. Madhu and Digumarti Bhaskara Rao, Editors (2006), *Psychological Adjustment and Well-being.* New Delhi: Discovery Publishing House. ISBN 81-8356-204-3.

Prasad Babu, B., Author and M.V.R. Raju and Digumarti Bhaskara Rao, Editors (2006), *Behavioural Problems of School Children.* New Delhi: Discovery Publishing House. ISBN 81-8356-206-X.

Prabhakaram, K.S., Author and Digumarti Bhaskara Rao, Editors (1998), *Concept Attainment Model in Mathematics Teaching.* New Delhi: Discovery Publishing House. ISBN 81-7141-424-9.

Prasanth Kumar, J., Author and Digumarti Bhaskara Rao, Editor (1998), *Effectiveness of Distance Education System.* New Delhi: Discovery Publishing House. ISBN 81-7141-437-0.

Prasanth Kumar, J., Author and Digumarti Bhaskara Rao, Editor (2004), *Methods of Teaching Civics.* New Delhi: Discovery Publishing House. ISBN 81-7141-806-6.

Prasanth Kumar, J., Author and G. Sundara Rao and Digumarti Bhaskara Rao, Editors (2000), *Open University Student Support Services*. New Delhi: Discovery Publishing House. ISBN 81-7141-550-4.

Raja Kumari, M.A. and D.R.S. Sundari, Authors and Digumarti Bhaskara Rao, Editor (2004), *Special Education*. New Delhi: Discovery Publishing House. ISBN 81-7141-846-5.

Raja Kumari, M.A. and D.R.S. Sundari, Authors and Digumarti Bhaskara Rao, Editor (2004), *Methods of Teaching Educational Psychology*. New Delhi: Discovery Publishing House. ISBN 81-7141-820-1.

Ramatulasamma, K., Author and Digumarti Bhaskara Rao, Editor (2002), *Job Satisfaction of Teacher Educators*. New Delhi: Discovery Publishing House. ISBN 81-7141-655-1.

Rama Krishnaiah, D., Author and Digumarti Bhaskara Rao, Editor (1998), *Job Satisfaction of College Teachers*. New Delhi: Discovery Publishing House. ISBN 81-7141-438-9.

Rama Kumar Ratnam, M.V., Author and Digumarti Bhaskara Rao, Editor (1998), *Dukkha: Suffering in Early Buddhism*. New Delhi: Discovery Publishing House. ISBN 81-7141-653-5.

Rama Krishna Prasad and P. Vide Sagar, Authors and Digumarti Bhaskara Rao, Editor (2004), *Methods of Teaching Physical Education*. New Delhi: Discovery Publishing House. ISBN 81-7141-868-6.

Rama Seshaiah, P. Author and Digumarti Bhaskara Rao, Editor (2004), *Methods of Teaching Home Science*. New Delhi: Discovery Publishing House. ISBN 81-7141-916-X.

Rama Swamy, K., Author and Digumarti Bhaskara Rao, Editor (2007), *Techniques of Teaching Environmental Science*. New Delhi: Sonali Publications. ISBN 81-8411-035-9.

Ramesh, A.R., Author and Digumarti Bhaskara Rao, Editor (2006), *Techniques of Teaching Commerce*. New Delhi: Sonali Publications. ISBN 81-8411-043-X.

Ramesh, Ghanta and Digumarti Bhaskara Rao, Editors (1998), *Environmental Education : Problems and Prospects*. New Delhi: Discovery Publishing House. ISBN 81-7141-423-0.

Ranga Rao, B., Author and Digumarti Bhaskara Rao, Editor (2007), *Techniques of Teaching Economics.* New Delhi: Sonali Publications. ISBN 81-8411-056-1.

Ranga Rao, R., Author and Digumarti Bhaskara Rao, Editor (2004), *Methods of Teacher Teaching.* New Delhi: Discovery Publishing House. ISBN 81-7141-812-0.

Rani, S.S., Author and Digumarti Bhaskara Rao, Editor (2006), *Techniques of Teaching Botany.* New Delhi: Discovery Publishing House. ISBN 81-8411-037-5.

Rathaiah, Lavu and Digumarti Bhaskara Rao, Editors (1996), *International Innovations in Education.* New Delhi: Discovery Publishing House. ISBN 81-7141-359-5.

Rathaiah, Lavu and Digumarti Bhaskara Rao (1997), *Achievement Correlates.* New Delhi: Discovery Publishing House. ISBN 81-7141-385-4.

Ravi Krishna, M., Author and Digumarti Bhaskara Rao, Editor (2004), *Examination System.* New Delhi: Discovery Publishing House. ISBN 81-7141-824-4.

Ravi Kumar, M., Author and Digumarti Bhaskara Rao, Editor (2004), *Methods of Teaching Computer Science.* New Delhi: Discovery Publishing House. ISBN 81-7141-823-6.

Rudramamba, B., Author and Digumarti Bhaskara Rao, Editor (2003), *Problems of Teaching.* New Delhi: APH Publishing Corporation. ISBN 81-7648-462-8.

Rudramamba, B. and V. Lakshmi Kumari, Authors and Digumarti Bhaskara Rao, Editor (2004), *Methods of Teaching Economics.* New Delhi: Discovery Publishing House. ISBN 81-7141-900-3.

Sambasiva Rao, P., Author and Digumarti Bhaskara Rao, Editor (2007), *Techniques of Teaching Psychology.* New Delhi: Sonali Publications. ISBN 81-8411-040-5.

Sanjeeva Rao, P.C., Author and Digumarti Bhaskara Rao, Editor (1996), *A Text Book of Geology.* New Delhi: Discovery Publishing House. ISBN 81-7141-313-7.

Santhanam, T., B. Prasad Babu and S. Sugandhi, Authors and Digumarti Bhaskara Rao, Editor (2007). *Children with Learning Disabilities.* New Delhi: Sonali Publications. ISBN 81-8411-077-4.

Santhanam, T., B. Prasad Babu and S. Sugandhi, Authors and Digumarti Bhaskara Rao, Editor (2008), *Learning Disabilities and Remedial Programmes.* New Delhi: Discovery Publishing House. ISBN 978-81-8356-257-7.

Sarala, M.M.O., Author and Digumarti Bhaskara Rao, Editor (2006), *Techniques of Teaching English.* New Delhi: Sonali Publications. ISBN 81-8411-047-2.

Satya Narayana, G., Author and Digumarti Bhaskara Rao, Editor (2008), *Attitude towards Social Studies and Achievement in Social Studies.* New Delhi: Sonali Publications.

Satya Narayana, V., Author and Digumarti Bhaskara Rao, Editor (2001), *Physical Education, Social Attitudes and Leadership Qualities.* New Delhi: Discovery Publishing House. ISBN 81 7141-593-8.

Satya Narayana, P.V.V. and G. Krishna, Authors and Digumarti Bhaskara Rao, Editor (2004), *Curriculum Development and Management.* New Delhi: Discovery Publishing House. ISBN 81-7141-813-9.

Shamsuddin, Sk. and V. Dayakara Reddy, Authors and Digumarti Bhaskara Rao, Editor (2007), *Values and Academic Achievement.* New Delhi: Discovery Publishing House. ISBN 81-8356-283-3.

Singh, Y.C., Author and Digumarti Bhaskara Rao, Editor (2006), *Techniques of Teaching Science.* New Delhi: Sonali Publications. ISBN 81-8411-041-3.

Sirisha Rani, S., Author and Digumarti Bhaskara Rao, Editor (2007), *Techniques of Teaching Botany.* New Delhi: Sonali Publications. ISBN 81-8411-037-5.

Sivaratnam Reddy, M., Author and Digumarti Bhaskara Rao, Editor (2004), *Creativity in College Students.* New Delhi: Discovery Publishing House. ISBN 81-7141-697-7.

Siva Lakshmi, G.V. and G.L. Subbaiah, Authors and Digumarti Bhaskara Rao, Editor (2004), *Methods of Teaching Environmental Science.* New Delhi: Discovery Publishing House. ISBN 81-7141-839-2.

Srinivas, G. and Digumarti Bhaskara Rao (2007), *Anxiety of Prospective Teachers.* New Delhi: Sonali Publications. ISBN 81-8411-084-7.

Srinivas, G. and Digumarti Bhaskara Rao (2011), *Intelligence and Personality of Prospective Teachers.* New Delhi: Discovery Publishing House. ISBN 978-93-5056-101-0.

Srinivas, M. and I. Prasada Rao, Authors and Digumarti Bhaskara Rao, Editor (2004), *Methods of Teaching History.* New Delhi : Discovery Publishing House. ISBN 81-7141-803-1.

Srinivas Rao, P., Author and Digumarti Bhaskara Rao, Editor (2007), *Principles of Secondary School.* New Delhi: Sonali Publications. ISBN 81-8411-058-8.

Srinivasulu, K., Author and Digumarti Bhaskara Rao, Editor (2011), *Achievement Motivation and Academic Achievement of Alcoholic and Non-alcoholic College Students.* New Delhi: Discovery Publishing House. ISBN 978-93-5056-063-1.

Srinivasulu, Kopperla and Digumarti Bhaskara Rao (2011), *Achievement Motivation, Academic Achievement and Alcoholism.* Saarbrucken, Germany: LAMBERT Academic Publishing GmbH and Co. KG. ISBN 978-3-8465-9296-0.

Srinivasulu Reddy, M. and K.R.S. Sambasiva Rao, Authors and Digumarti Bhaskara Rao, Editor (1999), *A Text Book of Aquaculture.* New Delhi: Discovery Publishing House. ISBN 81-7141-482-6.

Srinivasa Rao, Mandalapu, Author and Digumarti Bhaskara Rao, Editor (2003), *Achievement Motivation and Achievement in Mathematics.* New Delhi: Discovery Publishing House. ISBN 81-7141-674-8.

Srihari, M., Author and Digumarti Bhaskara Rao, Editor (2003), *Values of Prospective Teachers.* New Delhi: Discovery Publishing House. ISBN 81-8356-328-7.

Subba Rao, K., Author and Digumarti Bhaskara Rao, Editor (2007), *School Education Policy.* New Delhi: Discovery Publishing House. ISBN 81-8356-285-X.

Subba Rao, K., Author and Digumarti Bhaskara Rao, Editor (2007), *Education Planning.* New Delhi: Sonali Publications. ISBN 81-8411-053-7.

Subramanyam, N.R., Author and Digumarti Bhaskara Rao, Editor (2011), *Effectiveness of In-service Training Programmes*. New Delhi: Discovery Publishing House. ISBN 978-93-5056-078-5.

Sudhakar Reddy, Y., Author and Digumarti Bhaskara Rao, Editor (2003), *Creativity in Adolescents*. New Delhi: Discovery Publishing House. ISBN 81-7141-659-4.

Sunil Kumar, K. and K. Rama Krishana, Authors and Digumarti Bhaskara Rao, Editor (2004), *Methods of Teaching Chemistry*. New Delhi: Discovery Publishing House. ISBN 81-7141-913-5.

Suneetha, G., Author and Digumarti Bhaskara Rao, Editor (2004), *Environmental Awareness of School Students*. New Delhi: Sonali Publications. ISBN 81-8411-085-5.

Sunita, E. and R. Sambasiva Rao, Authors and Digumarti Bhaskara Rao, Editor (2004), *Methods of Teaching Mathematics*. New Delhi: Discovery Publishing House. ISBN 81-7141-915-1.

Surya Madhava, I., Author and Digumarti Bhaskara Rao, Editor (2006), *Techniques of Teaching Geography*. New Delhi: Discovery Publishing House. ISBN 81-8411-034-0.

Surya Madhava, I., Author and Digumarti Bhaskara Rao, Editor (2007), *Techniques of Teaching Political Science*. New Delhi: Discovery Publishing House. ISBN 81-8411-061-8.

Swamy, K.R., Author and Digumarti Bhaskara Rao, Editor (2006), *Techniques of Teaching Environmental Science*. New Delhi: Discovery Publishing House. ISBN 81-8411-035-9.

Swarna Jyothi, K., Author and Digumarti Bhaskara Rao, Editor (2007), *Educational Research*. New Delhi: Sonali Publications. ISBN 81-8411-063-4.

Swarna Latha, C.D., and Digumarti Bhaskara Rao, Editors (2006), *Encyclopaedia of Biotechnology*, 5 Volumes. New Delhi: Discovery Publishing House. ISBN 81-8356-168-3.

Swarupa Rani, T. and J.R. Priyadarshini, Authors and Digumarti Bhaskara Rao, Editor (2004), *Educational Measurement and Evaluation*. New Delhi: Discovery Publishing House. ISBN 81-7141-859-7.

Vanaja, M., Author and Digumarti Bhaskara Rao, Editor (1999), *Inquiry Training Model.* New Delhi: Discovery Publishing House. ISBN 81-7141-515-6.

Vanaja, M., Author and Digumarti Bhaskara Rao, Editor (2004), *Methods of Teaching Physics.* New Delhi: Discovery Publishing House. ISBN 81-7141-867-8.

Vanaja, M. and N. Sneha Latha, Authors and Digumarti Bhaskara Rao, Editor (2004), *Student Shyness.* New Delhi: APH Publishing Corporation.

Valeri V. Koustiouk, Author and Digumarti Bhaskara Rao, Editor (2002), *A Text Book of Cryogenics.* New Delhi: Discovery Publishing House. ISBN 81-7141-642-X.

Vamsi Krishna, V., Author and Digumarti Bhaskara Rao, Editor (2004), *School Psychology.* New Delhi: Discovery Publishing House. ISBN 81-7141-880-5.

Veena Kumari, Balusu and Digumarti Bhaskara Rao (1996), *Operation Black Board.* New Delhi: APH Publishing Corporation. ISBN 81-7024-711-X.

Veena Kumari, Balusu, Author and Digumarti Bhaskara Rao, Editor (2004), *Methods of Teaching Social Studies.* New Delhi: Discovery Publishing House. ISBN 81-7141-899-6.

Veena Kumari, Balusu, Author and Digumarti Bhaskara Rao, Editor (2000), *Psycho-Social Correlates of Achievement.* New Delhi: Discovery Publishing House. ISBN 81-7141-547-4.

Venkata Rao, B., Author and Digumarti Bhaskara Rao, Editor (2007), *Techniques of Teaching Chemistry.* New Delhi: Sonali Publications. ISBN 81-8411-057-X.

Venkata Rao, P. and Digumarti Bhaskara Rao (1989), *A Text Book of Zoology – Junior Intermediate.* Guntur: Vignan Publishers.

Venkata Rao, P. and Digumarti Bhaskara Rao (1989), *A Text Book of Zoology – Senior Intermediate.* Guntur: Vignan Publishers.

Venkateswara Rao, V., Author and Digumarti Bhaskara Rao, Editor (2004), *Problems of Education.* New Delhi: Discovery Publishing House. ISBN 81-7141-841-4.

Venkateswara Rao, V., V. Vijaya Lakshmi and V. Vamsi Krishna, Authors and Digumarti Bhaskara Rao, Editor (2004), *Education For All.* New Delhi: Sonali Publications. ISBN 81-88836-30-3.

Venkateswara Rao, V., V. Vijaya Lakshmi and V. Vamsi Krishna, Authors and Digumarti Bhaskara Rao, Editor (2004), *Education in India.* New Delhi: Sonali Publications. ISBN 81-88836-858-9.

Venkateswara Reddy, L. and Narayana, M. L., Authors and Digumarti Bhaskara Rao, Editor (2004), *Education for Dalits.* New Delhi: Discovery Publishing House. ISBN 81-7141-872-4.

Venkateswara Reddy, L. and Narayana, M. L, Authors and Digumarti Bhaskara Rao, Editor (2004), *Methods of Teaching Rural Sociology.* New Delhi: Discovery Publishing House. ISBN 81-7141-811-2.

Venkateswarlu, K. and S.J. Basha, Authors and Digumarti Bhaskara Rao, Editor (2004), *Methods of Teaching Commerce.* New Delhi: Discovery Publishing House. ISBN 81-7141-808-2.

Venugopala Rao, K., Author and Digumarti Bhaskara Rao, Editor (2000), *Teacher Morale in Secondary Schools.* New Delhi: Discovery Publishing House. ISBN 81-7141-551-2.

Venugopala Rao, K., Author and Digumarti Bhaskara Rao, Editor (2007), *Techniques of Teaching History.* New Delhi: Sonali Publications. ISBN 81-8411-059-6.

Vidya, C., Author and Digumarti Bhaskara Rao, Editor (1996), *A Text Book of Nutrition.* New Delhi: Discovery Publishing House. ISBN 81-7141-309-9.

Vimala, T.D., B. Prasad Babu and Digumarti Bhaskara Rao, Editors (2007), *Stress, Coping and Management.* New Delhi: Sonali Publications. ISBN 81-8411-086-3.

Vijaya Bharathi, D., Author and Digumarti Bhaskara Rao, Editor (2000), *Educational Philosophies of Swami Vivekananda and John Dewey.* New Delhi: APH Publishing House. ISBN 81-7648-309-9.

Vijaya Bharathi, D., Author and Digumarti Bhaskara Rao, Editor (2005), *Educational Philosophy of John Dewey*. New Delhi: Discovery Publishing House. ISBN 81-8356-024-5.

Vijaya Bharathi, D., Author and Digumarti Bhaskara Rao, Editor (2005), *Educational Philosophy of Swami Vivekananda*. New Delhi: Discovery Publishing House. ISBN 81-8356-023-7.

Vijaya Lakshmi, D., Author and Digumarti Bhaskara Rao, Editor (2004), *Basic Education*. New Delhi: Discovery Publishing House. ISBN 81-7141-881-3.

Vijaya Lakshmi, V., Author and Digumarti Bhaskara Rao, Editor (2006), *Techniques of Teaching Music*. New Delhi: Discovery Publishing House. ISBN 81-8411-038-3.

Vijaya Kumar, S.J., Author and Digumarti Bhaskara Rao, Editor (2006), *Techniques of Teaching Mathematics*. New Delhi: Sonali Publications. ISBN 81-8411-039-1.

Visalakshi, V., Author and Digumarti Bhaskara Rao, Editor (2006), *Techniques of Teaching Biology*. New Delhi: Sonali Publications. ISBN 81-8411-045-6.

Visalakshi, V., Author and Digumarti Bhaskara Rao, Editor (2007), *Techniques of Teaching Zoology*. New Delhi: Sonali Publications. ISBN 81-8411-055-3.

Books in Telugu Language

Bhaskara Rao, Digumarti (1986), *Dhrushya Sravana Bodhanapakaranalu* (Audio Visual Teaching Aids). Guntur: Nagarjuna Publishers.

Bhaskara Rao, Digumarti (1993), *Jeevasashtra Bodhana* (Teaching of Biology). Guntur: Nagarjuna Publishers.

Bhaskara Rao, Digumarti (1995), *Vignanasasthra Bodhana* (Teaching of Science) Guntur: Nagarjuna Publishers.

Bhaskara Rao, Digumarti (1994), *Vidya Manovignana Sastram* (Educational Psychology). Guntur: Nagarjuna Publishers.

Bhaskara Rao, Digumarti (1997), *Vidya Manovignana Sastram* (Educational Psychology). Guntur: Creative Press.

Bhaskara Rao, Digumarti (1998), *DSC Study Material*. Guntur: Nagarjuna Publishers.

Bhaskara Rao, Digumarti (1998), *Upadhyayudu Vidya*. (Teacher and Education) Guntur: Nagarjuna Publishers.

Bhaskara Rao, Digumarti (1998), *Vidya Drukpadalu* (Perspectives of Education). Guntur: Nagarjuna Publishers.

Bhaskara Rao, Digumarti (1999), *EdCET Teaching Aptitude*. Guntur: Nagarjuna Publishers.

Bhaskara Rao, Digumarti (2001), *Bharata Samajamulo Upadyayudu Vidhya* (Teacher and Education in Emerging Indian Society). Guntur: Sri Nagarjuna Publishers.

Bhaskara Rao, Digumarti (2001), *Bhoutika Sastra Bodhana Padhatulu* (Methods of Teaching Physical Science). Guntur: Sri Nagarjuna Publishers.

Bhaskara Rao, Digumarti (2001), *Jeeva Sastra Bodhana Padhatulu* (Methods of Teaching Biology). Guntur: Sri Nagarjuna Publishers.

Bhaskara Rao, Digumarti (2001), *Vidya Manovignana Sastram* (Educational Psychology). Guntur: Sri Nagarjuna Publishers.

Bhaskara Rao, Digumarti (2003), *Patasala Yajamanyam/ Paripalana* (School Management and Administration). Guntur: Sri Nagarjuna Publishers.

Bhaskara Rao, Digumarti and M. Srihari (2009), *Vardamana Bharata Desamulo Vidya* (Education in Emerging India). Guntur: Sri Nagarjuna Publishers.

Bhaskara Rao, Digumarti and B. Prasad Babu (2009), *Vidya Manovignana Sastram* (Educational Psychology). Guntur: Sri Nagarjuna Publishers.

Bhaskara Rao, Digumarti and B. Prasad Babu (2009), *Pradhamika Vidya mariyu Vileena Vidya Dhrukpadhalu* (Perspectives in Primary Education and Inclusive Education). Guntur: Sri Nagarjuna Publishers.

Bhaskara Rao, Digumarti and K. Subba Rao (2009), *Elementary Vidya, Pranalika, Yajamanyam, Upadyaya Kartavyalu* (Elementary Education, Planning, Management and Teacher Functions). Guntur: Sri Nagarjuna Publishers.

Bhaskara Rao, Digumarti and G. Prasanthi (2009), *Samardya Nirmanamu* (Capacity Building). Guntur: Sri Nagarjuna Publishers.

Bhaskara Rao, Digumarti and A. Jagadish (2009), *Vignansastra Bodhana Padhatulu* (Methods of Teaching Science). Guntur: Sri Nagarjuna Publishers.

Bhaskara Rao, Digumarti, Editor (2010), *Vardamana Bharata Desamulo Vidya – Question Bank* (D.Ed. Education in Emerging India). Guntur: Sri Nagarjuna Publishers.

Bhaskara Rao, Digumarti, Editor (2010), *Vidya Manovignana Sastram – Question Bank* (D.Ed. Educational Psychology). Guntur: Sri Nagarjuna Publishers.

Bhaskara Rao, Digumarti, Editor (2010), *Pradhamika Vidya mariyu Vileena Vidya Dhrukpadhalu – Question Bank* (D.Ed. Perspectives in Primary Education and Inclusive Education). Guntur: Sri Nagarjuna Publishers.

Bhaskara Rao, Digumarti, Editor (2010), *Elementary Vidya, Pranalika, Yajamanyam, Upadyaya Kartavyalu – Question Bank* (D.Ed. Elementary Education, Planning, Management and Teacher Functions). Guntur: Sri Nagarjuna Publishers.

Bhaskara Rao, Digumarti, Editor (2010), *Samardya Nirmanamu – Question Bank* (D.Ed. Capacity Building). Guntur: Sri Nagarjuna Publishers.

Bhaskara Rao, Digumarti, Editor (2010), *Ganithasastra Bodhana Padhatulu – Question Bank* (D.Ed. Methods of Teaching Science). Guntur: Sri Nagarjuna Publishers.

Bhaskara Rao, Digumarti, Editor (2010), *Vignansastra Bodhana Padhatulu – Question Bank* (D.Ed. Methods of Teaching Science). Guntur: Sri Nagarjuna Publishers.

Bhaskara Rao, Digumarti, Editor (2010), *Sanghikasastra Bodhana Padhatulu – Question Bank* (D.Ed. Methods of Teaching Social Studies). Guntur: Sri Nagarjuna Publishers.

Bhaskara Rao, Digumarti, Editor (2010), *Telugu Bodhana Padhatulu – Question Bank* (D.Ed. Methods of Teaching Social Studies). Guntur: Sri Nagarjuna Publishers.

Bhaskara Rao, Digumarti, Editor (2010), *Methods of Teaching English – Question Bank*. (D.Ed.) Guntur: Sri Nagarjuna Publishers.

Bhaskara Rao, Digumarti, Editor (2011), *Vidya Adhralu – Question Bank* (B.Ed. Philosophical Foundations of Education). Guntur: Sri Nagarjuna Publishers.

Bhaskara Rao, Digumarti, Editor (2011), *Vidya Manovignana Sastram – Question Bank* (B.Ed. Educational Psychology). Guntur: Sri Nagarjuna Publishers.

Bhaskara Rao, Digumarti, Editor (2011), *Vidya Sanketika Sastrm – Computer Vidya – Question Bank* (B.Ed. Educational Technology and Computer Vidya). Guntur: Sri Nagarjuna Publishers.

Bhaskara Rao, Digumarti, Editor (2011), *School Management – Systems of Education – Question Bank* (B.Ed. School Management and Systems of Education). Guntur: Sri Nagarjuna Publishers.

Bhaskara Rao, Digumarti, Editor (2011), *Personality Development and Communicative English – Question Bank* (B.Ed. Personality Development and Communicative English). Guntur: Sri Nagarjuna Publishers.

Bhaskara Rao, Digumarti, Editor (2011), *Ganithasastra Bodhana Padhatulu – Question Bank* (B.Ed. Methods of Teaching Science). Guntur: Sri Nagarjuna Publishers.

Bhaskara Rao, Digumarti, Editor (2011), *Bhoutikasastra Bodhana Padhatulu – Question Bank* (B.Ed. Methods of Teaching Physical Science). Guntur: Sri Nagarjuna Publishers.

Bhaskara Rao, Digumarti, Editor (2011), *Jeevasastra Bodhana Padhatulu – Question Bank* (B.Ed. Methods of Teaching Biological Science). Guntur: Sri Nagarjuna Publishers.

Bhaskara Rao, Digumarti, Editor (2011), *Sanghikasastra Bodhana Padhatulu – Question Bank* (B.Ed. Methods of Teaching Social Studies). Guntur: Sri Nagarjuna Publishers.

Bhaskara Rao, Digumarti, Editor (2011), *Telugu Bodhana Padhatulu – Question Bank* (B.Ed. Methods of Teaching Social Studies). Guntur: Sri Nagarjuna Publishers.

Bhaskara Rao, Digumarti, Editor (2011), *Methods of Teaching English – Question Bank.* (B.Ed.) Guntur: Sri Nagarjuna Publishers.

Bhaskara Rao, Digumarti, N. Saraja, J. Lalitha and V. Mrunalini, Translators (2008), *Vidya – Samajam (Education – Society). Hyderabad*: Dr. B. R. Ambedkar Open University.

Gopala Krishna, G., A. Rama Krishna, K. Subba Rao and Bhaskara Rao, Digumarti (2004), *Jeevasashtra Bodhana Padhatulu* (Methods of Teaching of Biological Science). Guntur: Sri Nagarjuna Publishers.

Krishna Murthy, V., K.S. Sudheer Reddy and Digumarti Bhaskara Rao (2004), *Vidya Manovignana Sastra Adharalu* (Foundations of Educational Psychology). Guntur: Sri Nagarjuna Publishers.

Lalini, V., V. Dayakara Reddy, M. Srihari and Digumarti Bhaskara Rao (2004), *Vidya Adharalu* (Foundations of Education). Guntur: Sri Nagarjuna Publishers.

Sastry, G.E.P. and G. Satya Narayana, Authors, Bhaskara Rao, Digumarti, Editor (2009), *Sanghikasastra Bodhana Padhatulu* (Methods of Teaching Social Studies). Guntur: Sri Nagarjuna Publishers.

Subba Rao, K.P., P. Ayodhya and Digumarti Bhaskara Rao (2004), *Patasala Yajamanyam – Vidhya Vyavasthalu* (School Management and Systems of Education). Guntur: Sri Nagarjuna Publishers.

Sudhakar, V., B. Ravindra Babu, D.S. Kumar and Digumarti Bhaskara Rao (2004), *Vidya Sanketika Sastram – Computer Vidhya* (Educational Technology and Computer Education). Guntur: Sri Nagarjuna Publishers.

WEBLIOGRAPHYWEBSITES

http://www.eric.ed.goc/ERIC web portal/search/detailmini.jsphttp://www.eric.ed.goc/ERIC web portal/search/detailmini.jsp

http://ww.sciencedirect.com/sciencehttp://ww.sciencedirect.com/science

http://ww.jstor.org/pss.2645089http://ww.jstor.org/pss.2645089

http://environment.harvard.eduhttp://environment.harvard.edu

http://www.environspace.comhttp://www.environspace.com

http://www.ir-doc.orghttp://www.ir-doc.org

http://environment.about.com/library/week/blgloss.http://environment.about.com/library/week/blgloss.

http://www.eco.potal.comhttp://www.eco.potal.com

http://www.edutechindia.orghttp://www.edutechindia.org

http://vis.unesco.orghttp://vis.unescho.org

http://www.ibe.unesco,org/internationalhttp://www.ibe.unesco,org/international

www.google.com (Environmental Awareness in India) www.google.com (Environmental Awareness in India)

www.yahoo.com (Environmental Awareness in India) www.yahoo.com (Environmental Awareness in India)

www.education.nic.in

http://www.cee.greenteacher.org (for educators) http://www.edutechindia.org

http://www.cee.kidsgreen.org (for children) http://www.edutechindia.org

www.education.nic.inwww.epa.govt.www.epa.govt.

www.eeweek.orgwww.eeweek.org

www.wwfechina.orgwww.wwfechina.org

www.wcs.orgwww.wcs.org

http://www.eurojournals.com/ajsr.htm

www.wikieducator.org/images/b/bd/PID_337.pdf

www.staff.um.edu.mt/ppac1/RDC17/limerick3.pdfURL:http://scialert.net/abstract/?doi=rjes.2011.77.81

INDEX